TRAIL MARKERS

TRAIL MARKERS

Life, Leadership, and Leaving a Spiritual Legacy

Berry Simpson

Editor: Bob Hartig
Interior design:
Cover design: Darrell Dunton, Admarc

ISBN-13: 9780983140078
ISBN-10: 0983140073

This book is dedicated to
Cyndi Simpson—*you make me a happy man.*
The Iron Men—*for the many hours we've spent together on the trail.*

Contents

Acknowledgments

I want to say thanks to two of the people who made this book possible:

Bob Hartig from Hastings, Michigan, who edited my text and offered many recommendations that made this book much more readable. Over and over I have been amazed at how well he knew what I meant to say, better than I actually said it. You can find him at thecopyfox.com.

Darrell Dunton with Admarc in Midland, Texas, who has been a friend and loyal reader for a long time. He encouraged me to turn my essays into books and kept pushing me to make sure it really happened. He has also designed the covers for all of my books.

Thanks,
Berry Simpson

Introduction

Buffalo Bill once said, "I could never resist the call of the trail." Well, neither can I.

I love trails. I wish I had more opportunities to run, hike, and bike on dirt trails; I seldom miss squeezing trail time into my schedule whenever I get the chance. I enjoy the unpredictability of a trail versus a city sidewalk, maybe because my life is routine and predictable (admittedly by my own making).

I started working on this book because I was fascinated by the idea of trail building. I even bought a Forest Service trail building manual to read their expert opinions. I spent months writing my thoughts on trail guides and ministry.

Trails are irresistible invitations to the unknown. A trail that disappears into the woods or climbs a ridge or curves around an outcropping is a trail I fall for. I have to try it out. I want to see where it goes.

Where the most beautiful backcountry seems impenetrable and inaccessible, a trail is an invitation to give it a try. A trail makes hiking the most impassable terrain a possibility. Having a trail to follow is a gift. It means you don't have to bushwhack. It tells you that you are not on your own.

A trail means someone has prepared the way for you. Someone you'll never know built this trail, maybe decades ago. So even when hiking alone, you are hiking with someone unseen, the trail builder.

Merely having a trail doesn't mean the hiking will be easy. You still have to climb the switchbacks, go down the ravines, avoid the rocks, and skip over the roots. But you are not lost. You have a path to follow.

Once, while running on a portion of the Continental Divide Trail near Vallecitos, New Mexico, I passed through a section where someone had cut a three-foot section from a big fallen tree to make the trail passable. They couldn't move the entire tree, or perhaps they didn't want to move it, but they opened a way through. *Here's the way through, man, come this way.*

When hiking in the wilderness, every step we take leaves a mark on the trail and helps to define it for those who follow. A trail seldom used becomes overgrown and lost to the surrounding terrain. Every hiker becomes a trail builder, a trail guide, simply by walking. Other hikers who come later, those we'll never meet, will follow our footprints.

Building a trail is an act of faith—faith that someone someday will use it.

God once told his people to leave an intentional trail for the next generation to follow on their way back home. He was speaking through the prophet Jeremiah at a time when the Israelites were being carried away into exile in Babylon. God wanted them to know the captivity wouldn't last forever; a day would come when they could return home. Jeremiah 31:21 says, "'Set up road signs; put up guideposts. Take note of the highway, the road you take.'"

God told the Israelites to make sure they could find their way home when the time came to return. This was not about wishing and hoping but actively setting up road signs, guideposts, bringing a map. The people had some responsibility to find their way back home. It was their obligation to be trail guides to the next generations.

In my early years I followed the clear and obvious trail left by my family. They were consistent, dependable followers of Jesus, and the path they blazed through life was easy to see and follow, hard to lose. As I got older and more of life's choices were mine to make, I needed new guides to show the way. Once again God put people in my path who served as trail markers, delineating the best way to live, reminding me I was still on the correct trail. And today, I know that I have become one of those trail markers for many others. It isn't an obligation I take lightly; it is the most important thing I do.

Being a trail guide means being entrusted with people, entrusted with the trail itself, and it turn entrusting my own guys with belief and insight and calling. A trail guide is less a mentor and more like a fellow traveler—as in, we are in this together.

> **The goal of trail building is to create a long-term relationship between humans and nature.**[1]
>
> **—PATHWAYS TO TRAIL BUILDING**

Some of the most useful trail markers are rock cairns: those man-made piles of stones used for hundreds of years to mark trails.

Rock cairns are intentionally stacked to mark a path.

Rock cairns are built to guide those who follow.

Cairns allow us to trust those who went before.

They help us discover the trail when we're lost.

They confirm we're still on the trail when we *aren't* lost.

Rock cairns are not passive; they must be maintained.

Even when a hiker knows he is on the right trail, knows she isn't lost, knows where he is on the map, coming across the next cairn is comforting and reassuring.

Keeping rock cairns alive is not a passive activity. They must be maintained and restacked and added to by generations of hikers to repair the daily damage from wind, rain, and animals. In the same way, keeping our life stories alive is not passive. It takes work. The stories have to be told often to be kept alive.

Not only are rock cairns cool to look at, but they describe how men should help each other to find calling, purpose, and meaning.

Rock cairns are proof positive that we are not alone. Stacking rocks as we pass tells those behind us they aren't alone either.

> **It's the wilderness trail, not the superhighway, that gets us to discovery.**
>
> **—JERRY GODDARD**

Thinking about these trail markers made me realize that I had been stacking rocks for a long time. I'd often found myself retelling the same old stories to Cyndi, over and over—the stories about our early days together, and how we found each other, and how we fell in love. It was like stacking rocks one on another, building rock cairns to show the path we took, the way we came, so we wouldn't forget, and maybe so others could follow.

Whenever I tell the same story, again . . . whenever I revisit a place to renew my memories . . . I am stacking rocks

Cairns remind us that we are obligated to pass on what we've learned to mark the trail for those who will follow.

Trail markers are the signs left behind showing us the way to go. In the wilderness, the most frequent markers are rock cairns. In our life, these markers are people we choose to follow, trail guides. They are the kind of l leaders who hike with us and show us the way.

Hikers don't want to follow rock cairns built by first-timers. Suppose you are trekking across new country and come across two trails. One trail is marked with rock cairns built by a Cub Scout troop and the other with cairns built by seasoned back-country Forest Service professionals. Which trail would you want to follow home?

> *It takes deliberate and sustained effort to build big cairns like that. Builders have to carry rocks from long distances as the close ones are used. The really big ones, I remember seeing big ones on the ridgeline trail to Truchas, require a ladder to get the rocks up on top.*
>
> —*BERRY*

This book is the result of my long journey of discovery: how to give away what's been given to me; how to live a significant life.

I didn't write because I understood my topic but because I needed to. I needed to learn and explore what it means to be a trail guide in the twenty-first century.

I wish this book's structure were more linear; that would make me more comfortable. Instead I have a collection of ideas that I hope will, when blended with your own stories, form a picture that encourages you to join me as a fellow trail guide. I ask you to hike the trail beside me and absorb what God has given.

Plenty of sources exist for learning how to live a significant life. Books, blogs, podcasts—most include step-by-step instructions. But nothing of value happened in my life as a result of such regimented actions. The most important, life-changing events seemed random and accidental, on the fly.

So I'm not going to give you Steps to Significance. I'm going to share stories that illustrate how God worked in my life and how God used my life to change others. I hope that as you read, your eyes will be opened to God's work in *you*. I hope you will relax and let him do his work. And I hope you will decide to live a deeper life with God.

> *Trails help humans make sense of a world increasingly dominated by automobiles and pavement. They allow us to come more closely in touch with our natural surroundings, to soothe our psyches, to challenge our bodies, and to practice ancient skills.*[2]
>
> **—WOODY HESSELBARTH**

Part 1: Trailhead

At a trailhead, the path to the future is laid out before you, inviting you in. However, only the beginning is visible; little else, if anything, can be observed past the first couple of turns.

I was fortunate to have my own personal guides show me the trailhead and the best way to go.

1

My First Marker

The nurse asked if I had medical power of attorney on behalf of my dad, and I nodded my head. "In fact, I'm using it. Back at his retirement village, we've already started selling his stuff."

She couldn't stop laughing, even though we were in the emergency room, and even though my dad was lying between us on a stretcher with various hospital machines attached to him. He had been cracking jokes at the expense of the nurse since arriving, and I just added to the mix.

Dad came home from the hospital that very same day with a diagnosis of vertigo. One of his best friends says, "We've all had that one. It's really a diagnosis of being old."

I give my dad full credit for showing me how to find the joke in any situation, to be funny without hurting other people, and to let the other guys get the big laugh. It's one of the most important things he gave me.

I don't know if my dad gave much thought to passing along the good things he learned. I'm sure it was important to him, but he's not from a generation or of a personality as introspective as mine, so it wasn't something he talked about.

Me, I think about it all the time. I seldom have a thought that doesn't run home to the question, How do I share what I've learned. How do I speak to the hearts of the young couples and the young men God has placed in front of me? How do I give away what was invested in me in the first decades of my life? What does that look like in the twenty-first century?

The apostle Paul was concerned about the same thing when he wrote to his young protégé, Timothy, "What you heard from me, keep as the pattern of sound teaching, with faith and love in Christ Jesus. Guard the good deposit that was entrusted to you—guard it with the help of the Holy Spirit who lives in us" (2 Tim. 1:13–14).

There is a progressive deepening of ownership in those verses. First we *hear* something. Then, because what we heard is important, we decide to *keep* it. At some point, keeping it isn't enough; we need to *guard* it and make sure to follow it. Finally, once we realize the information came to us not because we were lucky or smart but because God *entrusted* it to us, we are obligated to give it away.

So, sitting beside Dad while he slept in the emergency room, I remembered back in 2008, when I took him hiking on Guadalupe Peak to celebrate his eightieth birthday. It was not an easy hike. The National Park Service website describes this trail as strenuous and very steep, with exposed cliff edges. But we had a great time. The day was clear and sunny and never hot—a perfect day for hiking in Texas. We had fun on the trail telling jokes and wisecracks.

It took us two hours to hike up to The Notch, my first goal of the day. I wanted to get past this point so Dad could experience the tall pine trees and oaks and junipers. I wanted him to know there was more to this hike than the harsh, rocky switchbacks you see from the parking lot.

We hiked another hour and a half before stopping for lunch, just around the bend from the wooden bridge. We had hiked three miles and climbed two thousand feet, but we still had one mile and a thousand feet to the summit. After we finished our sandwiches and trail mix, Dad said, This is it for me today. I think we should go back down.

I said, You're right. It would be the wise thing to do.

He said, I'm having a great day, and I would love to make it to the top and phone my friends from the summit, but I don't want to be foolish about this.

I said, You know, if a teenager hikes too far and too long and blows all his energy and ends up stumbling home in the dark, it's a funny story.

If guys our age (fifty-two and eighty at the time) do the same thing, it's just stupid. It isn't a funny story, it's just stupid. We're supposed to know better.

So we started back down, which is easier than going up but never as quick as you imagine it will be. The thing about hiking a long trail is, when you get tired, there is no shortcut home. You can't sit on a rock and wait for the park rangers to wander by and give you a ride back to the parking lot. You just have to keep walking, no matter how exhausted you are. By the time we got down to the parking lot, we'd been on the trail for seven and a half hours, all of it hard work. We were whipped.

I asked, Was it a good day?

He said, It was a great day.

Even though I was the trail guide that day, my dad was still teaching me. You don't have to fight all the way to the top to have a good day.

There are so many things I give my dad credit for—things that have turned out to be fundamental characteristics of my life.

Besides humor, there was music. My dad was a church worship leader (back then we called them choir directors) as far back as I can remember. Not only did I learn to love and play church music, but I also learned from his example that music was something men could do. It was a manly activity, as much as hunting or carpentry. I don't know if I would've picked that up from anyone else.

Another thing I learned from my dad was that being a consistent man of faith for an entire lifetime is a noble, worthy, and courageous way to live.

Back in my university days in the late 1970s, one of my spiritual leaders, Chuck Madden, described how he was mentored by Leroy Eims of the Navigators. They lifted weights together every morning, went running, worked on writing books, and so on. There was no structure or step-by-step plan, just the rubbing off of personality and spiritual depth from constant exposure.

That's how I learned from my dad. That's how Timothy learned from the apostle Paul. One man rubs off on another.

I was blessed to be born into a family that loved and honored God. It was a blue-chip Baptist family, riddled with preachers, musicians, deacons, women's leaders, and solid church attendees. My parents and grandparents built deep and permanent faith in me, not by lecturing or preaching but by character and lifestyle and consistency, and by just daily rubbing off.

Maybe I would've found Jesus on my own. Maybe not. It doesn't matter. I didn't have to find Jesus on my own. I was shown the path to Jesus all my life.

Is the life I'm inviting other people to live, the life I'm living myself?[3]

—JOHN ORTBERG

2

Stepping Up

It was in my junior year at the University of Oklahoma that I first started asking hard questions about my faith. For the first time in my life, I was surrounded by people who were my age but who had different backgrounds. Some were believers like me, but from different traditions with different practices and terminology. Some believed in God but called him different names, some of which I couldn't come close to pronouncing.

Some believed in strange things like Transcendental Meditation, or Sun Young Moon; others claimed they didn't believe in any deity whatsoever and thought people who did had committed intellectual suicide. The argument that spiritual solutions hold answers for problems of the day caught very little traction at university in the late 1970s. So it was only natural that I would begin to question my own faith. What made my inherited beliefs more correct than my study companion's inherited belief in Allah or my roommate's inherited belief in atheism?

My questioning and research and skepticism brought me back to God, however, and this began the next stage of my life—a stage dominated not by my parents' faith but my own faith, earned from searching and deepened by spiritual disciplines. I learned to memorize Bible verses and Bible passages, do Bible studies, pray, share my faith, and disciple other students. And eventually all that learning changed me. It turned my life toward a deeper knowledge of Jesus, changed my heart, and gave God tools to speak to me.

I joined a campus group called the Baptist Student Union, and their structured program of personal discipleship and spiritual disciplines fit me perfectly. I was ready to step up and step in. Those disciplines, and my intentional embrace of them, changed my faith from something I inherited to something I owned.

Even after college, spiritual disciplines defined my spiritual life. I carried memory verse cards around with me everywhere, even when running, and that practice turned running into spiritual experiences. Then when I started teaching adult Bible study classes, it was about study and learning and reading and teaching. My habits became a study in spiritual disciplines, which dominated my thoughts and actions through decades of my adult life.

> **When you are living in your passion, people around you who were once sleeping will be woke up.**[4]
>
> **—ALLISON VESTERFEST**

3

Teaching

My first attempt at teaching was leading a Bible study in the dorms at The University of Oklahoma. A young man, Ray Tuttle, who was about two years ahead of me in school, took me under his wing, began spending time with me, and asked me to help him conduct his dorm Bible study. Mostly, as his helper, all I did was sit and watch. But we used study guides with printed questions, so I diligently worked on my own lesson every week to be ready in case Ray needed me to fill in, and because I assumed that was what I was supposed to do.

After Ray graduated and moved away to Chickasha, Oklahoma, to begin his career as a newspaper journalist, I took over leadership of the study. Because of the particular dorm we were working in, or maybe because of my own personality, the study had about a dozen very disciplined guys—engineering students, premed students, and military ROTC types. Most of them did their homework every week, and most participated in the group discussions. From the very beginning I was more comfortable in an open-discussion type of class rather than a lecture, but I was also comfortable being the leader, available to answer questions, guide the discussions, and be the last word on any controversies. I wanted lots of discussion, and I wasn't afraid of disagreements or nervous when the discussion took off chasing rabbits trails. I learned early how to bring everyone back to the point. I could use jokes and humor to keep the discussion light and put myself back in charge even when talking about very deep or serious subjects. I realized almost immediately that I had a gift and talent for this sort of teaching, and even more importantly, I had a heart to do it and a desire to get better.

After I graduated, Cyndi and I married and moved to Brownfield, Texas, and joined First Baptist Church and their couples' class. After about six months we were asked to attend a class designed to train new teachers. We were taught an overview of the entire Bible, some education theory, and classroom techniques.

Cyndi and I began to teach juniors and seniors in high school. We had a good group that took lots of trips. Cyndi and I went to camp and went skiing with them, and they babysat for us after Byron was born. It was fun even if a lot of work. We were established in leadership very early, running through three different youth ministers during our two-year tenure. Looking back it is scary to realize a couple in their midtwenties was the stability of the program.

> **Every young guy . . . wishes that some older man would come along and say, "I've got a revolution; we need you; follow me.**[5]
>
> **—BLAINE ELDREDGE**

4

Calling

I used to wonder about the Bible prophet Jeremiah. I was glad God didn't call me to be a preacher known as the "weeping prophet," crying over the nation's sins. Preaching against sin I could handle, but crying all day would be doubly hard for an analytic like me. Now I understand that God won't call us to something contrary to who we are.

Back in college, when the dorm Bible study leaders got together, my friend and fellow teacher Cathy Browning would tell about her girl's study and all the drama. She was always counseling, putting pieces back together, crying with her girls. I listened to her in amazement.

I told about my guys' study full of engineering and premed students who did all their class homework and were utterly devoid of drama.

Cathy and I just stared at each other and laughed. She would have suffocated in a class like mine, and I would have been desperate in a class like hers. I'd ask her, "How did all the emotional basket cases find you?" and she'd counter with, "How did all the brainiacs find *you*?"

When we finally learned about spiritual gifts, it opened up our world. God had given Cathy gifts to comfort and heal, and even if she didn't wear Master Healer label on her chest, the young women who needed her help found her. Her gift was like a magnet, pulling in those she was created to help. I remember Cathy and I laughing after our first exposure to spiritual gifts because at last the mystery had become obvious.

God calls us to places where we will fit, where our personality and gifts and passions can do the most good. He doesn't call us to places counter to who we are, as if to trip us up.

That doesn't mean the place he calls us to will be easy or come naturally to us right away. For one thing, our God-given calling gets covered up by the debris of life—by decisions, obligations, wounds and scars, and spiritual attacks—so that we may find ourselves struggling before the "real us" comes through.

Also, just because God plants our calling inside us and creates us to live it doesn't mean we won't have skills to learn and work to perfect. Being called by God means more effort, not less; it means more learning and training, not less. But when we're developing a skill that corresponds with our calling—whether it's teaching, speaking a foreign language, playing a musical instrument, or writing programming code—the learning process itself brings joy and fulfillment. It is not a burden. And people who need what we offer will be drawn to us even when they are unaware of the reason.

> **Even spiritual gifts are useful only in community. God gave them to us to build the church and serve each other, not to store up for ourselves.**

> **—BERRY**

Part 2: Trailcraft

There are skills, techniques, and attitudes a hiker learns along the way that make it possible to thrive on the trail. The more you learn, the farther you can hike, the deeper you can go, the harsher environments you can survive. Trailcraft translates to courage.

The only way to improve trailcraft is to practice on the trail itself. Reading and studying helps, but only disciplined practice under true life conditions, often under the eye of an experienced guide, stimulates permanent growth.

5

Practice

I spent a large portion of my second, third, and fourth decades immersed in the world of spiritual disciplines—things like Scripture memorization, daily Bible reading, writing and meditating, worship and church, teaching and study, and prayer. I started down that path for the same reason a young baseball player plays catch, attends batting practice, and lifts weights: to build skills that will make him a better player. To program physical reflexes and responses so that, in a game situation, doing the right thing comes naturally. In other words, to create instinct. I saw memorizing Bible passages in the same light: I was creating instinct.

I learned early that a regular practice of spiritual disciplines was essential to spiritual growth. And since a discipline is something we do in good times and bad, regardless of how we feel, practicing got me through multiple layoffs and injuries and illnesses. What surprised me, however, was that in the long run, practicing spiritual disciplines did more than make me smarter and more resilient. It created a relationship with God.

Too many followers of Jesus balk at the idea of spiritual disciplines, but why do they assume being a Christ follower is only one decision and then they're done? Why resist the idea that followers have to stay at it, have to "work out our salvation?"

An artist who doesn't paint for a long time will lose her creative edge, her unique viewpoint, even the muscles in her hand that allow her to work long hours. A teacher who takes time away from the classroom will lose the rhythm of teaching, the pattern, the insight into students, the "look" that makes the kids behave. A musician who stops practicing, singing or playing, will lose his gift. I still play my trombone, partly out of fear that if I put it away, it will be gone forever. I still play, but I don't do any quality practicing. As a result, I lose a little off my range and capacity every year. Even personal character fades unless it is fed and nurtured. And our relationship with God will fade into the background if we don't work it out.

Marathoner Alberto Salazar was a practicing Catholic his entire life, and in the later parts of his life he became more outspoken and deeper in his faith. He wrote about his faith in a book titled *14 Minutes* after a heart attack left him dead for that long. "I didn't see any white light when I died," he said, "but somehow my belief was strengthened. It requires faith to see God's hand. I don't regard faith as a passive virtue but as a praxis, a habit of heart and mind, which we build through effort and over time. . . . In my experience, miracles grow out of faith, and not the other way around."[6]

I've wondered why my fellow Baptists don't use the phrase "I practice Christianity" the same way a Buddhist would say, "I practice Buddhism." Catholics use the phrase "I am a practicing Catholic," but I don't think I've ever heard anyone say, "I am a practicing Baptist." I wonder why? I have heard people say, "I am a backsliding Baptist," so why not the positive side of that?

I think one reason we don't use the word *practice* is because we don't believe we earn our salvation; it is a free gift from God. So salvation isn't something we get better at; it came to us complete and whole and free, so we don't need to practice.

But our spiritual self will only grow if we maintain spiritual practices, and the Bible in fact encourages us to gather in community, pray regularly, learn the Scriptures, engage in fasting, and engage in other practices.

Salazar draws a line between salvation and faith. I think he is correct. We don't pray, "Increase my salvation," but we often pray, "Increase my faith." The idea that faith can be built over time by engaging in regular spiritual practices makes sense to me. In my own life, much of my relationship with God stems from the disciplines I learned and developed while at college and the Baptist Student Union.

My entire adult life I have been drawn to the notion of spiritual disciplines and practices.

Writer Natalie Goldberg defines *practice* as something you choose to do on a regular basis with no vision of an outcome; the aim is not improvement, not getting somewhere. You do it because you do it. Practice builds in us is a true confidence. This confidence comes simply from the fact that you show up over and over again.[7]

I started running in 1978 in order to win the heart of a girl and to lose weight and get fit. The girl (her name is Cyndi) married me. I kept running because I loved the dailiness of it and the escape from both people and social pressures. However, I ran hundreds of miles before I discovered the settling peacefulness. I had to push the barriers of discomfort and effort in order to find the mental release on the other side, to get to the fun part.

People often tell me they are inspired to run after reading something I wrote, but then they try a couple of times and give up because it was too hard. In fact, I don't expect other people to get the same thing from running that I get, and I don't think badly about them if they don't become lifelong runners. We are all drawn to different activities, and I don't expect anyone to be drawn to mine. Running is just an example; the point is, it takes consistent practice for a long time to change one's lifestyle.

Relationships are like that, too. Some couples can't stay together for more than a couple of months or a couple of years because all they know is discomfort and effort. They haven't stuck it out long enough to break through the barrier to the good side. It's as if God designed relationships to be frontloaded, like the Guadalupe Peak Trail, to see whether we have what it takes to keep going. Are we willing to stay at it until we hit the smoother flat parts?

For example, I have read through the same copy of my *Daily Bible*[8] almost every day since 1993. I started because someone told me to and I followed their advice. I kept at it because I wanted to deepen my relationship with God. My reason had changed: now I wanted to change who I was and how I lived so I could love God more.

Reading became a daily practice for me. And now that practice is as important as what I actually read. I do it because it is what I do. It grounds me. It brings me back home to my base relationship with God. It settles my wandering mind and keeps me from rambling too far from God's truth. The physical act of reading every day settles my mind and brings me peace. A day feels strange and empty until I have my reading.

So what is my point? I had to learn how to have a relationship with God. To my surprise, it requires a lot of time and effort and focus. Memorizing Bible passages hasn't made me a stronger guy, but has made me a better friend. Those passages and stories and insights have become the shared stories of our relationship—of God and me. Going through our "old stories" together over and over, year after year, glues us together the same way that revisiting old stories over and over with Cyndi bonds us. It is those shared stories that define us as a couple, and it is the shared spiritual experiences that define my relationship with God.

I have learned the value of getting away to go to Promise Keepers with my son, or Wild at Heart Boot Camp with Christian brothers, or even solitary backpacking trips in the mountains. I used to feel guilty if I came back from one of those trips without some new insights to share; otherwise, why invest the time? If I didn't learn something new and exciting and fresh to share with Cyndi and my Bible study class or write about in my journal, I felt like I had wasted my time and been self-indulgent with my money. I was wrong to think that way. Those focused spiritual experiences are not for leaving a new message as much as simply spending time with God. If I say I want more faith in God, I won't get it by more study or more facts; I'll get it by more relationship—spending more time with him and entering into his world.

***Insights unearned don't stick. It's our sweat and blood that proved the glue, preventing these wisps of clarity from floating off into space.*[9]**

—Eric Weiner

6

A Consistent Life

One Sunday in my adult Bible class, we discussed the famous story of Daniel in the lion's den. It is one of those stories more famous than the Bible itself—that is, even people who don't know the Bible know this story.

Daniel was a Hebrew serving at the top of the Babylonian government. He was trusted by the king, and it appears they had a close personal friendship. This stirred up jealousy among Daniel's rivals in government, and they conspired to get him in trouble and have him thrown out.

But they couldn't find any scandal or failure to pin on Daniel. Not one. Their only hope was to trip him up regarding his personal and consistent devotion to God. So they convinced the Babylonian king to make a decree that no one could worship anyone but the king himself, knowing this would trap Daniel. And it did.

Daniel 6:10 says, "Now when Daniel learned that the decree had been published, he went home to his upstairs room where the windows opened toward Jerusalem. Three times a day he got down on his knees and prayed, giving thanks to his God, just as he had done before."

Daniel merely repeated his daily practice of praying, and he got busted and sentenced to spending the night in the lions' den—certain death. However, God shut the mouths of the lions, they left Daniel alone, and he survived.

I contend that the story would be better served if the title were "Daniel in the Window" instead of "Daniel in the Lion's Den," because that would put the focus on Daniel's practice of prayer. The lions weren't as important as his daily disciplines.

Our spiritual self grows when we maintain spiritual practices: practice in the sense of regular, daily activities that we do for the purpose of doing them. They're more than mere rote or mechanical repetition. When I was younger, we called them spiritual disciplines, and the list included Bible reading, study, prayer, meditation, Scripture memorization, fasting, worship, and many more.

Even though it was miraculous that Daniel survived his night among the lions, he had little to do with it. He didn't use his ninja moves to fight off the lions. He didn't hypnotize them and put them to sleep. Daniel didn't climb the walls and stay out of reach. No, Daniel's strength, his "accomplishment," came from decades of devotion to God. Daniel was known for praying in his window several times each day. He didn't do it to attract attention or to show off but because his window faced Jerusalem. He prayed there because it reminded him of home and drew him to God.

Daniel had lost his family, his name, his culture, and his social net. Daniel became a eunuch when he entered government service, so he had no family of his own.

Daniel didn't even have a home to return to. Jerusalem, the center of his previous life and the representation of God on earth, had been leveled by Judah's war with Babylon. All Daniel had was a memory. So when he prayed, he prayed in a window that faced that memory, to connect him to God, to connect him to home.

The text says Daniel prayed every day, three times a day, for his entire life. It was that practice that gave him strength to endure. It was that practice that deepened his character so that king after king after king sought him out to serve in the upper echelons of government.

> **@berrysimpson: Why do running, cycling, hiking on dirt speak to my soul and spirit? Is it possible some things shouldn't be understood, merely practiced?**
>
> **@ctmcdm: [C. S.] Lewis says, "The surest way of spoiling a pleasure (is) to start examining your satisfaction."**

@berrysimpson: And so, that is the dilemma of being an analytic/mystic.

@ctmcdm: If we were Buddhists, the practice would be enough. But we must also tell our story, which requires introspection.

@berrysimpson: Maybe that's why I need to understand the process; I'm looking for the story.[10]

7

Not Disqualified

Most Wednesday and Friday mornings, Cyndi and I get out of bed at 5:00 a.m. to go to the gym for a one-hour weight-lifting class. I can't believe I get up so early—this is not who I am or who I hope to be or even my ideal of a perfect guy. I am, in my DNA, a night owl, and I would rather stay up all night reading than get up so early in the morning. The story I tell myself when the alarm goes off at 5:00 a.m. is that I won't be any happier getting up at 6:00 or even 7:00. And it's impossible to make an impact on the adult world the way I want to if I sleep in to the double figures every day.

One reason I get up so early on Wednesday is because that's the day Cyndi teaches, and I want to go to her class to support her and learn from her and watch her do something she's very good at. But as supportive as that sounds, I'm not really so noble. Cyndi has been teaching early morning classes of one type or another for most of our marriage, and I have almost never gone to any of them. Way back in the old days, I stayed home because one of us had to get the kids up and ready for school. Then in later years, I didn't go simply because I wanted to sleep instead.

For months I'd been trying to get fitter, build more muscle, and lose a significant amount of weight. Unfortunately, no one can schedule enough workouts using only the middle parts of the day. To reach my goal I had to inconvenience myself. As Erwin McManus wrote in *Wide Awake*, "You can't just sit back and hope that the life you long for will simply come to you."[11] Anything worthwhile is hard work and inconvenient.

This morning, as we went through the warm-up sequence with light weights, all of me—back, shoulders, legs, arms, knees, neck, hair—was stiff and gripey for being called into action so early. I had the same thoughts I've had during the first few moments of many road races, and many heavy backpacking trips, and every marathon: Why am I doing this? Who thought this was a good idea? Why can't I live a normal life that isn't so hard?

But after working through squats and clean-and-presses and triceps and biceps, well, I eventually tossed aside my doubts—probably because those thoughts were displaced by other thoughts of proper technique and pain management, but also because, at some point, I started to feel strong and mighty and lean and hard, in my own way, and then I was proud of myself for working so hard when most of my friends were still asleep.

And then, after an hour, we were done. We'd finished with abs and even with our cool-down. I was ready to go back home for a hot shower (or maybe to crawl back into bed for thirty minutes).

The apostle Paul wrote: "I discipline my body and make it my slave, so that, after I have preached to others, I myself will not be disqualified" (1 Cor. 9:27, NASB). To be honest, I don't know exactly what "disciplining my body" means. I doubt Paul went to weight-lifting classes. I think he probably was a runner at some point in his life because he wrote about it so much. But even more mysterious than Paul's workout discipline is, what did he mean that he would be disqualified? Disqualified from what? Preaching? Writing? Traveling? Mentoring?

Is it necessary to be physically fit to be a spiritual leader? We've all been influenced by teachers or preachers who weren't the least bit concerned with physical discipline, who were decidedly unfit and didn't care. They didn't seem to have been disqualified, so what did Paul mean about disciplining his body? I don't know.

But I do know that working out and running gives me a life with more choices. It means I can take a group of guys from my Bible study up Guadalupe Peak. I can join my band of brothers, the Iron Men, in an outdoor boot camp workout and share lives with them. I can walk seventy miles in one week, village to village, church to church, with John Witte in Karimoja, Uganda.

The most surprising thing is that I'm not good at any of this. I have no natural athletic skills; I run too slow, weigh too much, limp too often, and quit too soon. Yet I know that one of the reasons I can go backpacking or think about marathons or any of that is because of the strength I've built up from a lifetime of running and training. I hope to always be doing whatever I can do, whatever it takes, to keep from being disqualified to teach and preach and influence. That would be too much to lose.

8

Standing Firm

I was flying on Southwest Airlines to Detroit for a Noble Heart workshop when I read this in my *Daily Bible*, from 1 Chronicles 5:24: "These were the heads of their families: Epher, Ishi, Eliel, Azriel, Jeremiah, Hodaviah and Jahdiel. They were brave warriors, famous men, and heads of their families."

I don't normally spend much time reading Bible genealogies; usually I race through them. But since my purpose for attending the workshop was to move further into my role as a man for God, this particular list caught my eye. Who doesn't want to be like these men?

"They were brave warriors." Well, I want to be a brave warrior, knowing when it's my moment to stand up to the enemy.

"They were . . . famous men." I'll admit, I'd like to be famous too. A couple of years ago I received a public service award from the International Society of Petroleum Engineers for my time in city government and community projects. To receive worldwide recognition in front of so many nationalities and languages, and in front of Cyndi, was great. My tiny moment of being famous felt good.

"They were . . . heads of their families." Well, I've been a husband for thirty-six years, and a dad for almost thirty-five, so I can't avoid this. However, in the context of this passage, it means more than husband and dad: it means patriarch. And to be honest, while I certainly haven't sought this position out, I can see it happening more and more with each passing year. And not only one of the heads of my own family but, Cyndi likes to remind me, one of the heads of our church and community. I'm OK with that. I don't necessarily want to be the one in charge, but I definitely want to influence outcomes.

Here's the problem with those men from 1 Chronicles—their standing was trumped by what it says in the next verse, 25: "But they were unfaithful to the God of their ancestors and prostituted themselves to the gods of the peoples of the land, whom God had destroyed before them."

It's too bad. Men who could have changed the world for good wasted their chance by being unfaithful to God. And not that they just drifted away from God, but they actively gave themselves over—"prostituted themselves"—to the gods of the world, even gods they knew had been defeated.

What a waste. These men were brave warriors, well known and influential, men of importance, leaders, responsible, decision makers, yet they failed at the most important thing. Because of their unfaithfulness, God caused an enemy nation, Assyria, to swoop in and defeat them and carry all of them off as captives, spoils of war. Their families, friends, and neighbors suffered because these men failed to be faithful to God, their single most important task. In the final accounting, they did not have what it took.

It happens too many times. Good men in leadership positions, even influential spiritual leaders, twist off, start believing their own press clippings, and sell out completely to the god of this world. It's tragic.

So, finishing my flight to Michigan, I had to stop writing and return my seatback and tray table to the full upright and locked position. My final thought was this question: How do we keep 1 Chronicles 5:25 from happening to us?

Curiously enough, the very next morning, while drinking coffee on the porch at Sam's house, I read the following from Isaiah 7:3–9. God was giving instructions to Isaiah to be passed along to King Ahaz before a battle: "Say to him, 'Be careful, keep calm and don't be afraid. Do not lose heart because of these two smoldering stubs of firewood'" (the two attacking kings).

Here are the words we need to remember. God told Ahaz, "I've got this. You are in my hands. Don't lose heart just because your enemies appear scary on the outside." God also told him to be careful.

Those are good words. Just because we know God is with us is not time to be stupid, arrogant, or brash. We have to be careful. Take care. Think about what we do. Think about what we believe and whom we listen to.

Later, still in Isaiah 7, God said, "'If you do not stand firm in your faith, you will not stand at all'" (v. 9).

And there is the main point: If you don't stand firm in your faith, it matters very little what else you do. In fact, you won't stand at all.

Being careful means more than not making a stupid mistake in combat, or putting on armor and taking up weapons. Being careful means to stand firm in the faith.

We have to spend a lot of time and energy on the question, What brings me to God? When do I feel alive and connected to God?[12]

—Nancy Ortberg

9

Guard Your Heart

If Satan can harden our hearts, he can cripple our ministries, destroy our relationships, and sour our close communion with God. Satan attacks our hearts through overbooked schedules, too many important roles and assignments, people who irritate us and stir up our anger and resentment. We cannot hope to keep our heart open to God unless we take diligent action.

Proverbs 4:23 says, "Watch over your heart with all diligence, for from it flow the springs of life" (NASB). I have always thought of that verse in terms of guarding and protecting my heart—to diligently keep things away from my heart that might hurt it, might callous it, might tempt it, might break it. I thought of this in terms of staying tough and on guard.

But I also need to nurture my heart, keep it healthy, keep it alive. To do that requires me to be open and vulnerable, the opposite reaction from being on guard. It means to feed my heart and find ways to make it come alive. My heart is the source of my life, after all, for from it flow the springs of life. I don't want to go through life with a hard, tight, armor-plated, dead heart, but that is what I will end up with if I don't take action to diligently watch over it.

Erwin McManus compared guarding our heart to building core strength. Anyone who has worked out in the gym under an instructor for the past ten years, or read a magazine article about getting stronger, knows that everything comes from our core strength. In the fitness world, it is all about core strength training nowadays

I learned a big lesson about the importance of core strength when trying to nurse my aching knees. In fact, what I learned helped me to run the Dallas Half Marathon with Cyndi. Our original plan was to run with our daughter, Katie, as a family sort of thing, but then she got pregnant and wimped out of the race. So, it was just Cyndi and me (and four thousand other runners we didn't know).

I handled the distance better than I expected, considering my poor excuse for long training runs; I was beaten up and tired at the end but not defeated. One reason was because I've been training with Jeff Galloway's method: alternating running five minutes and walking one minute. It has helped a lot.

Galloway has been part of my overall scheme for recovering from injury, coping with seemingly permanent knee aches, and my strategy to keep doing this sort of thing for a few more decades.

He encourages runners to insert regular walking breaks into their running, whatever the distance. Galloway wrote, "When taken from the beginning of all long runs, walk breaks erase fatigue, speed recovery, reduce injury, and yet bestow all of the endurance benefits of the distance covered."[13]

I kept to my five/one schedule, making small adjustments whenever necessary to space my walking breaks with the water stops. I was able to start back running every time, and I maintained a better average pace than I would have had I tried to run every step. That is, until I got to ten miles.

At ten miles, I hit the wall. Maybe it was because that was the length of my longest training run; maybe it was just what happened that day. I don't know. But suddenly I just felt drained. I adjusted my pattern to running four minutes and walking one, but I still struggled. I eventually finished the half marathon by alternately walking a hundred steps and then running a hundred steps (my old backpacking trick). I wanted to finish in less than three hours, so I kept working hard. And I did finally finish in 2:55—an embarrassingly slow time to actually commit to paper and hard drive, but even at that, it was about twenty minutes better than my last half marathon in Austin. It is my recovery-era half marathon personal record Hopefully the first comeback in a new trend.

Prevailing is underrated. We tell stories about mighty acts of heroism and huge accomplishments, but prevailing probably accomplishes more. What was Frodo's most important skill? He prevailed. He didn't stop, he didn't give up, he kept going forward.

It is my only real skill as an athlete and the reason I have survived nine marathons. I am not a fast runner, never have been, but I prevailed nine times. It's true, I dropped out of two marathons, but nine finishes out of eleven attempts makes me happy, especially in an event I could never have imagined myself doing when I was young.

Back in 2005, when I first realized my left knee was hurt, I actually looked forward to surgery. I wanted a quick fix to put it back like it was. I was willing to put up with surgery if that's what it took to fix it in a hurry.

What I eventually discovered, thanks to my new friends at the Seton Clinic in Austin, was that instead of surgery I needed to increase my core strength. I followed a prescribed series of exercises every day to build my core strength and correct my muscle imbalances. It is a project I'll continue to work on for the rest of my life if I want to keep moving.

It's a similar story about our heart. We want quick fixes, weekend seminars, and fast solutions, but it takes a lifetime of guarding and feeding and protecting and building core strength to avoid heart injury. That is the "with all diligence" part.

Everything of value comes from the core. Everything comes from our heart. We have to go to our core and get stronger inside if we want to be productive and long lasting in our heart.

This is not a passive activity. We have to take the initiative to get stronger. We can't just hope or pray our heart will get stronger; we have to work it. We have to do the exercises.

We also have to eliminate the things that hurt us. What have I allowed to inform my life? Is it good? What have I allowed to shape my heart? Am I feeding my heart what it needs? What kind of crappyjack have I been eating?

Proverbs tells me to guard my heart, for it is the wellspring of life. God actually sees me as generative, able to create life. My heart is a wellspring; life can flow from me. This is way different than merely protecting what I have, or guarding what I know. or staying away from evil. This is not a defensive posture but an offensive posture. I am supposed to use my heart to create life in other people.

> **The purpose of spiritual disciplines is to deepen our relationship with Jesus so that he can continue to transform our lives. That's it.**[14]
>
> **—PATRICK MORLEY**

10

Slow Growing

Back in my university days, when I was studying to become an engineer, I had to take a variety of elective classes to broaden my experience. One was economics, which I passed with a couple of strategically timed all-nighters. Of course, just because I passed the class doesn't mean I remember much about economics. Anything I learned in those all-night sessions has frittered away except for "guns and butter" and "no free lunch."

It used to bug me that I couldn't pull an all-nighter training session and run a marathon the next weekend. No, I had to set aside weeks, months, of consistent training. I had to keep working it.

Why can't I become a faster, longer runner right away, like in the movie *Matrix*? Just plug the cable into my neck and upload endurance and speed. And why can't I become a better cyclist using the same technique?

Why can't I morph into a skinny-yet-strong flatbelly overnight? Why does everything I want to do, at least everything of value, take so long?

Erwin McManus wrote, "For our lives to be a work of art, we need to allow a lifetime of work ... We must press close to God ... We must be willing to take the time and risk the intimacy required for creating an artisan life."[15]

If we want to be valuable to God and to the people around us, we have to keep putting in the work to improve. George Sheehan wrote, "Training is not like money. You cannot put it in the bank and save it. You have to go out continually and fight again and again for the desired improvement."[16]

It turns out this is also true about relationships. Even the closest relationships die without constant attention. The most heartfelt "I love you" fades away from memory if it isn't repeated regularly.

It doesn't seem fair. Why is life that way?

Because humans leak. Just like the tires on my bicycle, which lose air slowly and will be completely flat if I don't add air each time I ride, we humans leak our hard-earned fitness, we leak our fought-for endurance, we leak knowledge about economics, and we leak the assurance that we are loved. And not only do we leak, but because we live in a fallen and broken world, we are constantly under attack by the voices that tell us to sit down and give up.

But here's the thing: it is the work itself that changes our lives. It is the long training sessions that change us from couch potato to athlete. It is the deep conversations with those we love that change our heart.

One of my favorite places to hike is the trail up to the summit of Guadalupe Peak. It's always a hard day. The hike is eight miles roundtrip, with a three thousand–foot increase in elevation. And since the trailhead is above 5,000 feet, I am out of breath just getting off the bus.

I've made this hike at least fifteen times, and about halfway up I usually remember that early on, there were plans to build a tram to the top. The tram would allow anyone to ride to the highest point in Texas and enjoy the view without having to complete the difficult hike. While I'm hiking, trying to protect my knees and struggling to breathe, the tram proposal seems a pretty good idea. But if we rode to the top, all we'd get for the day would be the view. We wouldn't experience the life-changing friendships born of shared struggle, or the strengthened self-image from a hard job well done, and we certainly wouldn't have any stories to share on the drive home.

Again, from Erwin McManus: "Artists understand that the process of fermentation cannot be rushed or hurried. They know that the products they are committed to creating will not happen if they take short cuts or circumvent the process."[17] (He was comparing our lives to baking bread.)

The coolest part of this is, I no longer see the idea of long-term training requirements as a bad thing. It doesn't frustrate me (as much). Because I know that if I keep working—working at running and cycling, working to improve my writing, working to be a better supporter and lover to Cyndi Simpson—I will be. For all of us, it means our future can be better and deeper. If we get to work.

> *The disciplines can increase our intimacy with God so that we can work to extend His reign in the lives of those around us.*[18]

—*Philip Nation*

11

Work It Out

Cyndi said she was having trouble one day getting her class of fifth graders to settle down and pay attention to math. "Oh, Mrs. Simpson, this is too hard. We don't want to do this," and like that.

She said, "Guys, you need to learn this. You don't want to grow up to be an adult and still be only fifth-grade smart."

It's the same with growing in Christ. We don't want to be an old Christian still thinking baby-Christian thoughts and leaning on baby-Christian faith.

Spiritual disciplines are not easy.[19]

—REBEKAH LERNER

In Paul's second letter to the Thessalonians, over and over he praised them for their hope, faith, and love, and then encouraged them to do more. He wanted them to increase, to grow, to have even more faith, hope, and love.

There are two ways to think about that. We could think about it like a healthy diet. If someone wants to stay healthy and fit they have to eat that way, and it never stays done. They have to eat healthy from now on, the rest of their lives. That can be so overwhelming for many people that they never even get started. Why do something so hard that doesn't stay done?

The fact it, the more consistent we are in what we eat and when we eat it, the more our discipline becomes habits, and eventually the struggle gets easier. Yet for many, the reward of an easier struggle someday isn't enough to sustain a change. They won't even try.

The Christian life can appear that way. Why learn to hope, and to show faith and love, like the Thessalonian church, only to hear someone like Paul come along and tell you to do more? Is that all we have to look forward to as Christians, always doing more? Isn't that a little frustrating?

Well, we can look at it as a bad thing that we will never arrive, never be good enough. Or we can look at it knowing we aren't stuck being the way we are today. We can get better. We can learn more. Our best days are always ahead of us—not because we'll never be good enough, but because we can keep getting better.

If we don't adopt that pattern, then we are stuck with the spiritual maturity we started with. Like Cyndi's complaining kids, we'll be grownups who are only fifth-grade smart.

The Bible says we should "work out [our] salvation" (Phil. 2:12), which causes heartburn among some readers because it sounds like we might have to work hard to be saved. Not true. Conversion happens when we encounter God himself through the saving grace of his Son, Jesus Christ. It is the encounter, not our performance, which saves us.

However, as a saved Christian, we have a lot of growing to do. As Paul wrote to the Ephesians, we should show ourselves worthy of our calling (Eph. 4:1). We don't have to earn our salvation, but salvation should motivate us to work hard on our lives to be worthy of Jesus's free gift.

Personally, I like the fact that I have more to learn, more faith to have, more hope and more love ahead of me. I like having room to grow. I am glad my best days are ahead of me, not behind me. In America we sometimes think the prime of our life was when we were young adults. As a believer, I believe the prime of my Christian life is tomorrow. I may make big mistakes today, but I'll be better tomorrow.

Arrange your time so that you are experiencing deep contentment, deep joy, and deep confidence in your everyday life with God.[20]

—John Ortberg

Part 3: Trail Guides

Some trails are so difficult we need guides to talk us through even before we begin the hike. The Guadalupe Peak Trail is one of those. The first hour is almost always hot. The trail is steep and hard, a series of rocky switchbacks that gain elevation step after step. You have to put your head down, stare at the trail, and just keep moving—a bit like daily life. There is no quick way to the top, no shortcuts, no secret passageways available to the really cool people.

Because so many first-time hikers stop their climb and turn around before passing the opening switchbacks, we have learned to give a small motivational speech before each group hike. We explain how hard the first part of the trail can be so that no one is surprised, but we also point out that the difficulty doesn't last all day. The trail will get easier, and prettier, so don't give up too soon.

12

Life-Changing Lessons

It was a Monday morning at IHOP, a rare treat for me, but I was feeling sluggish since I'd spent twelve-plus hours the previous day (and night) driving home from a men's weekend near Buena Vista, Colorado. However, I had the good fortune to share breakfast with an old friend, Max Barnett. He was the director of the Baptist Student Union when I attended the University of Oklahoma in the late 1970s, and his ministry changed my life.

It was under Max's guidance that I learned the importance of spiritual disciplines. Under Max I learned how to stand up in front of a large group of people and teach those same disciplines, and how to be a small-group Bible teacher. But more importantly, it was where I first heard God's call on my life to be a leader, a teacher, a mentor, a disciple maker. Seeing Max again was a great encouragement, especially following a great spiritual retreat in Colorado.

After breakfast, Cyndi phoned my office to ask how it all went. I think she was worried I might've fallen asleep in my pancakes. I told her, "It was wonderful. I just heard, once again, the core of my life."

I first heard Max's vision when I was twenty years old; hearing it again thirty years later reminded me of the strength and depth God has given me through the years. I thought of the great gift of solid teaching I received at such an impressionable time in my life, and the huge obligation I now feel to stand up tall and teach what I've learned.

Listening to Max reminded me of more than my past, however. It occurred to me that I was still learning those same lessons. In fact, my previous weekend in Colorado was another call from God to step into the ministry Max first birthed in me way back then.

The life of faith is dynamic. I've grown accustomed to the notion that my faith will change as I grow older, but I haven't always felt that way. I used to assume I would eventually settle into the truths of life. I had a vision of ticking off the boxes as I went along, one life lesson after another, carrying forward the truths I learned and never having to rethink those things again. As in, "There, I've learned that. Now I can move forward." As if my spiritual journey were a series of merit badges: once learned, always learned.

I don't expect that any more. Nowadays I expect constant change. I expect to know and believe different things ten years from now. I expect that if I follow Jesus for the next fifty years, my understanding of him will change year by year. If he asks me, "Who do you think I am," I expect my answer to change. I know that Jesus won't change—he is always the same yesterday, today, and forever. But my understanding of Jesus changes because my needs change, my world changes, my relationships change, and so what I need to see about Jesus changes. Some of that is circumstantial. My life will change in ways I cannot control, and my walk with Jesus will have to keep up.

But the most exciting aspect of all this is that I expect to change simply as an effect of faith itself. Leonard Sweet says, "Faith is kinetic and transformational."[21] Simply having faith in God will change me day after day. And it will change me in ways I cannot prepare for or anticipate. I can't train or study for such change; all I can do is hold on and enjoy the ride.

So over Monday morning pancakes, I was living in two worlds: in the world of change, fresh from my Colorado weekend and the new call from God, and also in the roots of my past. I heard the foundation of my life reiterated, still as fresh and vibrant as when I first heard it thirty years ago. I told Cyndi I could feel the molecules of my body vibrating sympathetically with Max's words as he cast his life's vision for us at IHOP.

We are called to apply the weight of our lives to the world around us. That morning reminded me how my weight arose. It was an amazing, refreshing, challenging, and renewing blessing. I am ready to keep learning, and I'm ready to keep sharing.

> *We often confuse genius with mastery. Genius is a gift we are given; mastery is the stewardship of our gifts.*[22]
>
> **—ERWIN MCMANUS**

13

Be Like Don

One Wednesday afternoon I sat in the worship center of First Baptist Church with many of my closest friends to say goodbye to a man who would not leave me alone.

The previous Sunday morning, as I was preparing to play my trombone with the church orchestra, my friend Hank tapped me on the shoulder and said, "Don passed away this morning." Don had been very sick and was getting sicker, so the news wasn't a huge surprise. Yet, I felt the loss immediately. Don was seventy-three. For such a quiet and unassuming man, he had a huge impact on my life.

I first met Don Bomar at the Good News Guys Reunion Group, a men's share group that met once a week on Thursdays to talk about our lives and how we were trying to live as Christians, so we could encourage, counsel, and pray for each other. Don earned the nickname DOB because he once confessed that as he drove to our meeting he realized he had nothing to share, so he decided to Drive On By.

I once told the group about my attempt to donate blood two days earlier. I was refused because my blood pressure was too high; I don't remember the actual diastolic and systolic numbers, but both were in the triple digits. Don quietly asked if I'd seen a doctor yet. I said no. Don phoned me the next day to ask if I'd seen a doctor, but I said no again. He called me every day until I made a doctor's appointment, then kept calling daily until I actually went to see the doctor, and then phoned every day until I had my prescription filled. He did not leave me alone.

Don's right hand didn't work well, I suppose from a stroke or illness that happened before I knew him. I never asked about it. I tried to remember to shake his left hand, but I forgot more times than I remembered. Sometimes Don would have to hold his right hand up with his left, a lot of trouble just to shake hands, but he did it smiling and with grace. I would be embarrassed that I'd failed to honor him by remembering, but he didn't seem to care.

It was impossible for me to sneak past Don, whether in the hallway at church or in some parking lot around town. He always tracked me down. Don would walk beside me, put his arm around me, and say, "I love you, man." He often followed me out to my pickup to tell me something he'd just read or heard on the radio, or he would quote my own blogs back to me. I was amazed he paid so much attention to what I wrote.

Don would ask me if I'd read a certain book, usually about current events or, more often, religion. Rather than asking again the next time he saw me, he might wait, but he always asked a second time. If I told him I still hadn't read it, he would ask if it was on my shelf (he knew I had a to-read shelf). The next time he saw me, he would be carrying a plastic bag from Barnes and Noble with a copy of the book in it, and he would give it to me. He'd say, "No, hurry, but after you read this, give me a report. I want to know what you think."

He did not leave me alone.

I saw Don every Thursday morning at Whataburger, and he'd always ask about my 6:30 a.m. Iron Men group. He knew I'd driven straight from church, and he wanted to hear my assessment while the class was still fresh on my mind.

After Don died, I liked to sit in his favorite booth while writing in my journal, hoping to channel a bit of his grace and humor. I hope I am like him when I grow up. I hope my heart is full of grace, like Don's. I hope my eyes sparkle with joy, like his. I hope I will be as gentle and kind when people shake the wrong hand or do the wrong thing. I hope I will always be as quick with a joke.

Don Bomar was a confirmation of how one gentle man can change lives around him. I am blessed to have had a friend like Don, who would not let me go, who took such great care of me. I want to be like him.

God has decided, for his own good reasons, that people are not transformed outside of community.[23]

—JOHN ORTBERG

14

Following Advice

Uncharacteristically, I did what someone else told me to do. Not right away—I stalled for a couple of years. Maybe four.

My ophthalmologist, Dr. Jeff Grigsby, wanted me to sleep wearing an eye patch. Why? Because since I was six years old I've slept with one eye open, a result of several surgeries on my eyelid, so my eye has a tendency to dry out and get irritated. My doctor felt that wearing a patch over the eye would keep me healthy longer. He recommended this every year for at least four years.

I knew he was right. He is a good friend, and I trust what he says. But I didn't want to sleep in an eye patch. It just seemed too bizarre. Too old-mannish. Too much Captain Ron.

But then, in an unpredictable move, while I was at Walgreen's shopping for first aid materials to treat a cycling wound, I added an eye patch to my kit. And the first time Cyndi left for the weekend, I tried wearing it. And then I wore it the second night.

And much to my surprise, those were the best two nights of sleep I'd had in, well, maybe ever. I never realized how much energy I was consuming during the night protecting my eye with my hand or my pillow. I was so used to taking care of it—it's been this way since I was about six years old, and I never realized it was causing me trouble.

The next time I visited Dr. Grigsby for my annual checkup and contact lens renewal, I had my eye patch in my pocket to show him how obedient I'd been. And to tell him he was right. He was pleasantly surprised that I had a patch and gracious about the outcome. He didn't even say, "I told you so." In fact, it was as if he was more concerned with helping me than he was about being right all along.

Here's the thing. I am good at following advice I already agree with. I can follow that sort of advice with no effort, almost without listening. It's much harder to follow advice from anyone who isn't like me. Or maybe I should say, anyone who isn't me.

After my eye patch experience, I wondered how many other things in my life burn up energy without my noticing because I've tolerated them so long they feel second nature? How much advice have I ignored because I'm determined to do things my own way—advice from people I know and respect and like—because I don't want to admit I need help?

I decided that going forward I would force myself into hearing from teachers who have different personalities than I do, just to open up my life. To keep it from becoming too small. My first opportunity was deciding to use Bob Goff's book, *Love Does*, in our upcoming Iron Men session. I had never taught from such a nonlinear book. That is why I picked it. I have all the linear reinforcement I need; I wanted to hear advice from a completely different quarter, a completely different pattern, with a completely different result. I don't know how much Goff will pull me off my straight-line life, but I'm open to considering some possible changes. After all, I'd been wearing this eye patch, and once you start sleeping like a pirate, who knows what will happen next.

Anyone who isn't embarrassed of who they were last year probably isn't learning enough.[24]

—ALAIN DE BOTTON

15

Be a Lifelong Student

I was thirty years old before I became a student. It wasn't until then that I understood the value of intellectual discipline, and I set about to learn how to think.

Before that I coasted on the data I learned and the experiences I had when I was younger. I had a rich spiritual upbringing thanks to family and church, and another deep infusion of spiritual truth while I was in college. I taught and lived from those past experiences and stories for too long.

Then I heard a set of cassette tapes by motivational speaker Jim Rohn. He was the first voice I heard that encouraged a systematic and intentional life of gathering and capturing knowledge. He asked, How many people keep a list of the books they read and a journal where they capture quotes and ideas? Very few. It will put you in the top 10 percent.

What he said changed my life. Not only did I start reading again, but I kept a list of books I'd read and started keeping a to-read shelf at home so I would have the next book ready. I started regularly checking the new-book section at our local library, and I'd grab anything that caught my attention regardless of topic or author. Mr. Rohn made me hungry to learn. I wanted to be in his top ten percent.

A few years later I took another hit from another teacher.

It was a Sunday evening and I was sitting in a metal chair taking notes from a lesson on church history taught by our pastor, Jim Denison. As I listened to Dr. Denison answer questions and dig deep into far-ranging topics, I realized two things: (1) he might be the smartest man I'll ever know, and (2) he hasn't stopped learning. He was teaching from fresh learning. He wasn't pulling out his threadbare notes from university days but giving from what he'd just learned. Jim was actually engaged in his own education, even as an adult, even though he already had a PhD. The light came on in my head; the gravitational pull of learning seized me. I decided that very evening that I wanted to be just like him and pursue knowledge, wisdom, and insight for the rest of my adult years.

As soon as class was over, I asked Dr. Denison for a reading list, and a few days later I received two lists—one with ten books about church history, and the other with ten books about theology. It was a killer list, too; seminary-grade reading. In fact, the list was a bit more than I'd planned. I worked hard tracking down books in that pre-Internet, pre-Amazon era. I learned how to use the interlibrary loan system. I wrote book reports and sent them to Jim, hoping to keep my reading honest and my study on track.

Why am I telling these old stories?

Because of something I read in Gordon MacDonald's book, *A Resilient Life*. He told about a time when he was caught unprepared as a young pastor. One of his church members was killed accidentally on a hunting trip, and MacDonald felt inadequate and spiritually dry trying to minister, with nothing to offer the family. He wrote, "It was a most miserable moment, a scary one for a youthful pastor. . . . I determined I would never again be caught with an empty soul when others needed spiritual resources."[25]

As I read MacDonald's story I realized I felt the same way. I don't want to be caught spiritually dry while trying to minister. The classes I teach need a teacher who is growing and learning right alongside them.

MacDonald wrote, "I came to see that I owed my congregation a filled-up soul."

Yeah, me too. I owe those God has entrusted to me a filled-up soul. I now see learning as an obligation. To do any less is to sacrifice the gift.

The mastery of our craft should be paramount, for without it we will never have the language to tell the full story of our lives. To leave our gifts and talents unmastered and undeveloped is to leave wrapped precious treasures entrusted to us.[26]

—ERWIN MCMANUS

16

My Own Bagger Vance

Looking back over more than twenty-five years of writing, I realize that understanding and communicating God's personal calling has been important to me for a long time, certainly since the beginning of my modern era. As far back as high school, I felt there was a call, a purpose, to my life, but I didn't understand it or know how to explore it. It was more of an ambient thought in the back of my mind that I was aware of but didn't know what to do with.

That is, until 2002, when a friend loaned me a set of cassette tapes. ("Here, this seems to be the sort of thing you would like.") The tapes were from a workshop by Gary Barkalow, who was with Focus on the Family at the time. Gary has since become my friend, but at the time, I'd never heard of him or his ministry. His workshop on God's will and calling was the freshest thing I'd ever heard. And I'd never heard anyone use video clips while teaching. I took notice how effective it was.

I was between jobs at the time, searching for the next thing and begging God for insight. To keep myself occupied, I was building bookshelves in my garage, so I listened to those tapes repeatedly while working, day after day. I had to make copies so I wouldn't wear them out before returning them to my friend. Besides the fact that I was actively seeking employment, I expect the reason Gary's message resonated so strongly with me was that it was something I'd been thinking for a long time but didn't know how to articulate.

Gary taught me that God was more concerned with our character than with our next job. He cared more about the path of our life than about our individual choices. He didn't have to change his perfect plan every time we made a bad decision because his perfect plan was to train us up, grow us up to be like Jesus, and he did that through all our decisions, whether good or bad.

Our calling from God was not about career or job. In fact, I had always assumed God had called me to be a petroleum engineer and a Bible teacher, and maybe a writer, but I learned that those were merely assignments, the tools God gave to put my calling into action.

All that information changed the way I taught and the content of every lesson from that day forward. I realized that God's call for me is to give away what I've learned—to share my heart, whether through engineering or writing or teaching. In effect, my call is to tell the story.

I realized that every lesson I taught, every essay I published, every conversation I joined, ended up focusing on one of these topics: growing closer to God every day, becoming a lifelong student, pursuing our love, or growing stronger in community. That was the story I had to tell.

I also had a desire to break down the barriers we Westerners erect dividing the spiritual life from the secular. I don't see a difference. I believe *everything* is spiritual, whether preaching or cycling, singing or backpacking, studying or running marathons.

I have been fortunate to be influenced by powerful men throughout my life, and it is my desire to be one of those men for the people around me.

As iron sharpens iron, so one person sharpens another

—Proverbs 17:17

17

Letting Go

I'm continually searching for the sweet spot to live my life in, the still point, the center. I assume I'm only one practice, one habit, or one spreadsheet away from blissful yet productive existence. That's one of the reasons I read so much, or at least, it's how I pick many of my books. I'm looking for ideas to find that intersection between stillness and adventure.

One of my favorite writers, Natalie Goldberg, described how she handles life's burdens, and the numbness that comes from constant disappointment, in her book, *The True Secret of Writing*. She adopted a personal mantra that she repeats to herself; she calls it her "Loving Kindness Practice":

May I be happy.
May I be peaceful.
May I be free.
May I have the ease of well-being.
May I be safe.
May I be healthy.[27]

Goldberg believes her own inner peace expands out to everyone and everything else when she repeats those phrases to herself. I'm sure she's correct.

She also wrote about the process of letting go—as in, what are the elements she has to let go of in order to live happy, peaceful, free, and healthy? What do we carry with us all the time? What should we carry from now on? What should we leave behind? Goldberg understood that it wasn't enough to simply repeat a mantra over and over. She had to let go to make her "Loving Kindness Practice" really work.

Like a backpacker, we can only carry so much. It's true that the more gear we carry, the better we protect ourselves from surprises and accidents. But if our load gets too heavy, it will break our back and destroy our will to continue down the trail.

I wondered if I could adopt a practice similar to Goldberg's, based on a biblical perspective. Even though the actual end result might be the same and the specific practices not that different, it made a difference to my heart if I knew the source.

Which led me to Galatians 5:22–23: "The fruit of the Spirit is love, joy, peace, patience, kindness, goodness, faithfulness, gentleness and self-control." Could I use this list to ground myself in God's qualities in such a way that they would expand out to everyone else around me?

So I am proposing the following practice based on the fruits of the Spirit, and I'm asking you for suggestions to make it even better. What if we all repeated at least one of these phrases to ourselves every day, all day? Would it change how we live? Would it change the people around us?

May I be accepting; let go of judging.

May I be generous; let go of cynicism.

May I be mindful; let go of my need for respect.

May I linger; let go of quick success.

May I be kind; let go of condemnation.

May I give slack; let go of my expectations of others.

May I be loyal; let go of grudges.

May I be gentle; let go of being right.

May I be intentional; let go of careless living.

So far, this list seems a little clunky to be sustainable, but it's a good start to a brighter and more contagious life. Why don't you join me by selecting one phrase every day and repeat it to yourself whenever life's disappointments hit. Who knows what may happen.

The problem with hoarding is, you end up living off your reserves. Eventually you will become stale. If you give away everything you have, you are left with nothing. This forces you to look, to be aware, to replenish. Somehow the more you give away the more comes back to you.[28]

—PAUL ARDEN

18

Stay in One Place

I was at a funeral for Helen Spinks, one of the lions of grace who have blessed my life. When I first started teaching adult Bible study classes in our church, Helen would grab me every Sunday and tell me, "I have been hearing great things about you." My heart would swell almost to bursting. As a new teacher, I needed to hear her words. I was a better teacher because of her.

When Cyndi and I were in our church's young-marrieds class and parenting two preschoolers, Helen hosted a group of young women at her house to teach calligraphy. In the process of practicing calligraphy, the women learned all sorts of things from Helen about how to live with a growing family and how to stay close to God.

Her funeral was held in the main worship center of First Baptist Church in Midland, and it was packed to capacity, with overflow into the chapel. It was full of people from different tribes, from family, from FBC, from Junior League, and on and on—all people who had been touched by Helen's life.

Afterwards, walking across the parking lot to my pickup, I asked God, "How do I live my life to impact that many people?"

I distinctly heard him answer me with, "You stay in one place a long time."

This happened in 1995, a desperate time in the oil and gas business. I was out of work and searching diligently for my next job. Maybe my next career.

The prospects of finding a job in the petroleum industry were bleak. I had been applying and interviewing for the previous year and made absolutely no progress. So I considered changing industries. I especially wondered about the new high-tech industries that were blossoming in California, Oregon, and Washington, so I subscribed to a want-ad clipping service for engineering jobs in those three states. I also subscribed for the same service in the Dallas-Fort Worth area. This was long before all job searches took place on the Internet, before social media, before LinkedIn, before online resumes.

But that day in the parking lot I heard God's unmistakable voice say, "Stay in one place a long time."

I knew immediately what that meant. Don't leave Midland. The only way to influence so many people, like Helen did, was to live consistently for Jesus, day after day, years after year, and stay in one place for a long time. Some godly people change churches so often, or move from town to town so often, they never make a lasting impact

After that parking lot conversation, I stopped sending resumes and determined to remain in Midland no matter what. I expected God to find my place here.

But it was scary to stop. I felt like I had already mined any and all job leads in Midland. I didn't tell Cyndi about the conversation and my decision to stop searching nationwide for a long time—not until months later, when I was again gainfully employed. Cyndi was frightened enough about our future, and I wasn't confident enough in my decision to add that to her pile of worries.

Nothing is more unnerving or disorienting than passionately pursuing God.[29]

—MARK BATTERSON

19

Equilibrium

My friend Paul Ross once told me his feet are happiest when standing on uneven ground. As a true Wyoming mountain man, living on level ground in Texas has taken its toll on him.

Me, I don't mind level ground so much. After all, I've lived in West Texas 86 percent of my life, and the other 14 percent was in places just as flat. Level ground comes natural to me.

For the longest time I saw the level landscape as a metaphor for life. A life well lived was smooth, even, and stable. In fact, I looked forward to the day when my whole life would be balanced; when I would be settled into my perfect job and perfect house and perfect pickup and perfect relationships and perfect ministry and perfect set of goals and dreams. A balanced life sounded good to me.

I remember mentioning to Cyndi about how living in balance was surely calm and peaceful. She pointed out that a ballet dancer balancing on point appears calm and graceful, but if you could see inside of her leg and foot you would see muscles firing with constant corrective movements. Cyndi thought there was no real perfect balance for humans. At least, not if the human was alive.

She's very smart. Not long after our conversation, I read this in a science book, *Deep Simplicity*, by John Gribbin: "Equilibrium is of no intrinsic interest because nothing happens there. . . . The nearest a living thing ever gets to equilibrium is when it dies."[30]

So if equilibrium equals death, then being alive must be unstable, unbalanced, and turbulent. The trick to surviving is to get better at the corrective movements. The older I get, the more comfortable I am living that way. Not only am I comfortable, I've learned I need change and surprise, even instability, in my life to keep growing and stay creative. I need a bit of turbulence in order to thrive.

Which brings me to something I read by Patricia Ryan Madson in her excellent book *Improv Wisdom*: "In the act of balancing we come alive ... Sometimes we feel secure, sometimes precarious. In the long run we develop tolerance for instability."[31]

A couple of summers ago, Paul took Cyndi and me on a long hike in the Rocky Mountains National Park above Estes Park, Colorado. We saw at least seven beautiful, serene lakes and dozens of mountain streams. It was amazing. For the entire day we were surrounded by stunning, snow-capped peaks, but for Cyndi and me, it was the water that caught our attention. We took more photos of running water than anything else. I'm surprised we didn't take any videos in order to capture the sound, since rushing water against logs and rocks, turbulent flow, is simply musical. We couldn't get enough of it.

Thinking about what it means to be a trail guide and mentor, I've wondered how this idea of balance and the desire to live a level life fits in. Should I encourage young men to find stability, or should I tell them to learn to, in the words of Ms. Madson, "embrace the wobble"? Does Jesus care whether we have equilibrium in our lives? Does he want us unbalanced?

I don't know. But I know this: Jesus wants us to live in whatever state causes us to seek after him. For me, that is not equilibrium, not balanced, not a steady state. It's a little bit wobbly. And I am getting used to that.

In my desire to be a mentor to men and a trail guide on our shared spiritual journey, my main responsibility is to show that life is *more*. I want to pull back the curtains of daily distraction and point out that there's more to this life than living and dying. There's more.

We are animals in our blood and in our skin. We were not born for pavements and escalators, but for thunder and mud.[32]

—JAY GRIFFITHS

20

Exposed

The climb up Tejas Trail is approximately four miles long and 3,000-foot elevation gain. It is tough under any conditions, and it's very hard work under a heavy backpack. On this trip I was carrying sixty-two pounds, almost half of it water. (My pack weighed only thirty-five pounds coming down two days later). But I have made the climb a dozen times with a similar load; this trip was nothing out of the ordinary.

I was hiking with David Nobles, and this was his first trip like this.

David and I left the trailhead at 12:30 p.m. and finally made it to our camp spots at Pine Top at 6:30. I typically take only four hours to make this hike, even with a fully loaded backpack, but this time I bonked. We spent an extra two hours on the trail because of me.

I was short-winded the entire day, even at the beginning where the trail is relatively flat. It was impossible to set a steady hiking pace because I stopped continually to catch my breath. I reverted to a pattern of two hundred steps and one hundred breaths almost the entire trail. Nothing like that had ever happened to me before. It was discouraging, disappointing, and irritating.

At one point I started feeling queasy in my stomach, and the queasiness eventually became nausea. As a precaution I moved my camera into my cargo pocket. It had been hanging from a lanyard around my neck for quick access, and when I bent over at the waist it hung strait down. I moved it so I wouldn't throw up on it if it came to that.

About three miles into the climb, I sat down on a rock and loosened my pack. David sat with me awhile until we worked out a deal. He hiked the rest of the way up to the crest, dropped his pack, then came back to help me. While he was gone, I pondered my sad state of being: How did it come to this? I remembered hearing an interview with Erwin McManus and he said everything looks like failure in the middle." Even though I knew better, this felt like failure.

It wasn't easy to be the man down. Having David carry my pack for me wasn't as embarrassing as I thought it would be, since I knew I was in trouble and wouldn't have made it to Pine Top before dark without his help. But it certainly wasn't what I had in mind when the day began.

Why was I so short-winded? I knew I wasn't dehydrated. And I wasn't hungry; I'd eaten a similar lunch and breakfast on all my hikes. Was the altitude affecting me? That seemed unlikely since I'd made this exact same trip with a heavy pack at least a dozen times and never experienced nausea or extreme short-windedness.

Realizing you are mortal is irritating. It's hard being the one who needs help. It didn't seem very leaderly. Of course I would've done the same for David had the roles been reversed, but I wasn't used to the roles being reversed. I like the roles the way they usually were.

As David carried my backpack up the trail, I thought about something Jesus said in Matthew 5:41, as rendered in the New Living Translation: "If a soldier demands that you carry his gear for a mile, carry it two miles." Jesus told us to serve each other, to give more than is asked of us. That's what David did for me. He did more than was expected or asked, and he got me to the top. Through the years, I've carried packs for others to help them, and now I watched someone carry mine. Carrying is more satisfying than watching.

But if all we do in life is carry for others, never watch them carry for us, that really isn't relationship. If all we do is give, never receive, we have to wonder about our motives. Are we truly serving the needs of others or feeding the needs of our own ego? We must be willing to receive if we expect to know the grace of God. Only empty-handed people can under-stand what it means to receive grace.

> **Be careful, keep calm and don't be afraid. Do not lose heart.**
>
> **—ISAIAH 7:4**

Part 4: First Summit

Reaching the summit of any climb is exhilarating. You have earned the right to stand on top of a mountain by hiking through the discomfort and fatigue, and you are often rewarded with a spectacular view.

Our daily walk with God is often hard and steep, but we have the map provided us in the Bible, and we have well-worn paths in front of us created by the feet of countless fellow searchers. But we won't experience the breathtaking view of his presence unless we do the hard work. It's up to us to start hiking and keep hiking until we reach the summit.

21

Teaching Again

When we moved to Midland, Texas, in 1982, we had two-year-old son Byron, and Cyndi was pregnant with Katie. We decided to join First Baptist Church and found a young couple's class filled with people like us. We intended to take a few months away from teaching, raise our family, listen to God, and learn our new place of ministry as young adults with a growing family before being pulled into a more permanent position.

The few months we took off from teaching turned into nine years. That's the problem with plans like ours.

Then one Sunday, while Keith Parker was teaching his class, I heard a clear voice in my head say, "*You should be teaching.*"

That's it. That's all it said. Very *Field of Dreams.* The voice was so clear and articulate, and so off the point of the lesson we were studying, that I knew it was from God. Later, when I told this story to Keith, he suggested it was God telling me to jump up right then and take over the class because he was doing it so poorly. But no, it was a bigger call than that. I knew even in the moment that God was calling me back to active duty, calling me to something I loved and knew I was good at. Something I had lazily put on the shelf for too long.

Later at lunch I told Cyndi the story of hearing the voice in class: "You should be teaching." She said, "Well, duh, everyone knows that." The way she said it sounded like the rest of our friends had been talking about this and agreed it was obvious. As if I was the last to know. Maybe I was.

But it didn't feel like Cyndi was making fun of me for being so slow, it felt more like she was endorsing the decision and agreeing to once again be part of a teaching team.

So the next Sunday I approached our Sunday school department leader and said, "I think I need to be teaching. Can you find a class for me?"

Marylyn Leonard must have already suspected something was up, because she didn't hesitate. She said she would see what she could find. As it turned out, they were in the process of creating a new department and we moved in as brand-new teachers, teaching married couples our own age, many of whom were in Keith's class with us the previous year.

It felt right the very first Sunday. Well, except that I taught the wrong lesson—the lesson intended for a month away. But besides that, it felt like I was at home. That was September 1990. For the next fourteen years, Cyndi and I taught our own peer group of married couples. Our class morphed from fifteen sitting in a circle to over fifty with me standing up in front. We developed many deep friendships through that group, many of whom are our best friends still today.

You've been sitting quietly for far too long![33]

—GANDALF

22

What I Was Born to Do

In 1 Corinthians 1:1, the apostle Paul described himself as "called to be an apostle of Jesus Christ by the will of God." I wrote in the margin of my Bible, "He is certainly confident of his position." As for me, I often choke on the phrase "called by God." I'm not sure I have a right to make that claim. I believe it intellectually but struggle with it practically.

It is easier for me to say, "I am a petroleum engineer," since I have a university degree to back it up. Easier to say, "I am a marathoner," since I have a collection of finish medals to prove it. Easier to say, "I am a deacon," or, "I am a teacher," since I have a certificate in my file cabinet and a class full of people. Now that I have published several books I can say, "I am an author," with confidence.

But to say, "I have been called by God" to teach or write is harder. Claiming to be called by God, as the apostle Paul did, assumes an endorsement by God and implies a level of skill and talent that seems presumptuous to claim for myself.

I doubt I'm alone in my reluctance. I imagine most people feel the same way I do. It is always easier to see God's calling on someone else's life than on our own.

More than one person in the Bible resisted being called by God. For example, Moses argued with God about his calling even while standing barefoot in front of the burning bush. You'd think the bush would've convinced him. And Gideon pulled a double stunt, the wet fleece/dry fleece bit, hoping to understand the call he feared. He's lucky he wasn't slapped down by the angel who gave him the message. And even though God called Jeremiah to be a prophet before he was born, as soon as he was old enough to object, Jeremiah said, "I don't know how to speak. I'm only a child."

Maybe some level of reluctance is a good thing. It's what keeps us leaning into God to fulfill the calling rather than using our own ego. Maybe the humble spirit God is looking for is hidden within that reluctance. That is, as long as reluctance doesn't turn into rebellion.

In a May 2010 sermon Erwin McManus asked, are you doing what you were born to do? Are you doing what you're doing on purpose?" If not, you're like a big log floating downstream wherever the current takes it, hanging up on brush, bumping into rocks, jamming with other logs. Understanding what God has called us to do demands that we act on it. No more drifting.

McManus quoted Ecclesiastes 10:10: "If the ax is dull and its edge unsharpened, more strength is needed, but skill will bring success." We all want to be the guy up front swinging the ax, but few have the discipline to sharpen their skills. Realizing your call from God can be frightening, since with great power and energy comes even greater obligation and expectation. We have to hone the skills God has given us.

You can't be content with mastery; you have to push yourself to become a student again.[34]

—AUSTIN KLEON

23

It's Hard to Wait

Cyndi and I spent a week in the Carson National Forest of northern New Mexico. Cyndi was attending a workshop, and I was hanging out with her. Our camp was deep in the Carson National Forest at the 8,000-foot elevation in the Tusas Mountains.

One morning, while running on a mountain trail through the woods and listening to a podcast, I heard a familiar Bible story. It was from the Old Testament, about the leadership transition that occurred at the end of Samuel's life. During the days of Israel's first kings, Saul and David, Samuel was the spiritual leader for all of Israel, spokesman for God, and the last of the national judges. The text reads: "When Samuel grew old, he appointed his sons as Israel's leaders. The name of his firstborn was Joel and the name of his second was Abijah, and they served at Beersheba. But his sons did not follow his ways. They turned aside after dishonest gain and accepted bribes and perverted justice" (1 Sam. 8:1–3).

I thought it ironic that Samuel's sons followed the same path as Eli's sons. Eli was Samuel's predecessor and mentor, and Samuel got his job because Eli's sons were so corrupt. You'd think Samuel would have learned something about wayward sons from watching Eli's family, yet here Samuel was facing the same problem with his own sons.

I wonder why he appointed them as Israel's leaders? Surely Samuel knew his sons were not up to the task. Was he blind to their corruption? Did he know about it yet appointed them anyway? Maybe he had no one else and didn't know what else to do, so he appointed them and hoped for the best.

The story goes on: "So all the elders of Israel gathered together and came to Samuel at Ramah. They said to him, 'You are old, and your sons do not follow your ways; now appoint a king to lead us, such as all the other nations have'" (8:4–5).

When the elders asked Samuel for a king, saying, "You are old and your sons are worthless," their unspoken charge was that Samuel had failed. He hadn't arranged for proper succession. He had let the nation down, and now they had no future, and it was all Samuel's fault.

One wonders why the elders of Israel didn't appeal to God first and ask him, "What are you going to do with these dishonest sons of Samuel? What is next for us?" Instead they asked for a king. God gave them freedom to decide their course of action, and they chose to be like all the other nations. It was peer pressure on a national scale.

Who knows but that they circumvented the will of God by asking for a king. Maybe God had a miracle planned for Samuel's sons that would turn them around. Or maybe he had another yet-unknown leader picked out whom he would call up as national priest, just like he did with Samuel to replace Eli's sons. But because these elders pushed their own agenda through Samuel and asked for a king without even praying about it, they had to settle for less than God's best.

As I ran on that mountain trail in New Mexico, I wondered, How often do I get impatient with God and push for my own agenda? As in, "The people in charge aren't doing a good job, I'm stuck with the goofy stuff they're doing. They don't deserve to be there and I'm just doing menial tasks that don't matter. I'm tired of all that, and I want something else." I am pretty sure I've prayed that exact prayer more than once in my career.

It would be easier to wait for God's solutions if we knew for sure what he was going to do and when he would do it. But that wouldn't be faith. Mark Batterson wrote, "Faith doesn't reduce uncertainty. Faith embraces uncertainty. . . . Faith has less to do with *gaining knowledge* and more to do with *causing wonder*."[35]

Last spring I accomplished one of my life goals: hiking the South Rim in the Big Bend National Park in Texas. On my second day in the mountains,

I hiked south on a mostly smooth trail that twisted and turned up and down the hills. I knew I was approaching the rim, which is a thousand-foot drop-off down to the desert floor, but I couldn't see anything of the famous view.

Until suddenly I could. In a matter of a few steps, I crested a small rise, and all at once I could see hundreds of miles deep into Mexico. It was breathtaking, and the original trail builders did their job well, creating a view that could be anticipated but not experienced in bits and pieces. I had to wait, trusting the map that eventually my long hike would pay off.

Jesus never promised security. He promised uncertainty. He didn't give his disciples any details, just told them to "follow me."

How many times have I pushed the wrong solution to a situation because I was in too big a hurry to wait for God to do it his way—and in his grace, he gave me my wish? Maybe his original path would have protected me from the unintended consequences that always seem to accompany my choices.

Do I circumvent God's best and miss his blessings when I'm wallowing in self-pity? I hope not. If I am willing to pray for God's will, something I do frequently, the I should also be patient for his will to unfold. It's hard to wait, but that is the essence of faith.

I run in the path of your commands, for you have broadened by understanding.

—PSALM 119:32

24

Perfect Timing?

There is a Bible story about God's perfect timing found in the Old Testament book of Deuteronomy, chronicling the Hebrew people's journey from Egypt to their new home. The second verse of chapter 1 in the Amplified Bible says, "It is [only] eleven days' *journey* from Horeb (Mount Sinai) by way of Mount Seir to Kadesh-barnea [on Canaan's border; yet Israel wandered in the wilderness for forty years before crossing the border and entering Canaan, the promised land]."

Don't let the strange names distract you. Pay attention to the numbers. Instead of eleven days, it took 14,600 days. It took 1,327 times longer than it should have. That is a frightening extension!

The reason it took forty years was their own fault: they chose to listen to ten fearful spies rather than God. But that isn't much comfort. I make way too many decisions of my own based on fear, so I know I'm not immune from the same fate. I've always hoped God will compensate for my lack of courage by taking up the slack instead of adding to the journey—but then, here is this story from Deuteronomy.

Granted, I don't expect God's journey to be quick and easy. As Jon Acuff wrote, "Journeys where the outcome is already known are not adventures, they're errands. And we were created to do more than run errands."[36] But a 1,327-fold increase? That is so far over the top it is incomprehensible.

The question I have to ask is this: Am I willing for my journey to take twice as long as I expect, or ten times longer, or 1,327 times longer, if that is what God requires to transform me and transform my message? Am I willing to write another forty years before ten thousand people will read one of my books? Will I patiently teach for forty more years before knowing how much of it sticks? Am I willing to write weekly journals for another forty years before I know whether anyone reads them?

The people spent forty years reshaping their national character, waiting for their turn, yet after all that, they were still a bit uncertain about when and where to go next. They had prepared long enough; they had fretted enough; it was time to advance. But it took God to prod them into action: "'You have stayed long enough at this mountain. Break camp and advance'" (Deut. 1:6–7).

One of the hardest things to know is when to advance. There is always something more to learn, a new skill to master, or resources to accumulate. I doubt I have ever felt "ready" for the next step of my life.

I certainly wasn't ready for fatherhood. I thought I was ready for marriage, but little did I know what it was really about. I wasn't ready for my first job, or my first management position. I certainly wasn't ready for my first day in city government. I have never been ready to run a marathon. I wasn't ready the first time I got laid off, wasn't ready to be self-employed. I wasn't ready to build a new house, wasn't ready to raise teenagers, wasn't ready to be full-time Uncle Berry, wasn't ready to lead Iron Men. Yet here I am. As with those Hebrews, forty years of training didn't seem like enough for me once I got to the border of decision. It took a push from God every time.

God said in Deuteronomy 1:8, "See, I have given you this land. Go in and take possession." Just because the moment of perfect timing has finally arrived doesn't mean the job will get easier. Just because God tells us to advance and promises that the future is ours doesn't mean we won't suffer casualties. We have to "take possession," a short phrase that may represent a lifetime struggle. Maybe forty more years.

One of the greatest mistakes we make in our spiritual journey is circumventing the process of accomplishing our God-given dreams by trying to achieve those dreams in a manner that violates God's character. Joshua was about to lead God's people into war, yet God's emphasis was on the quality of his character. Be strong, Have the courage to do what is right regardless of circumstance or consequence. Live a life of conviction.[37]

—ERWIN McMANUS

25

I Wasn't Ready

At a men's weekend at Crooked Creek Ranch in Colorado, Gary Barkalow talked about how we have to wait patiently for God to give us opportunities to use our gifts and talents and calling. Sometimes we might get passed over at a time we thought was perfect for us, or lose a chance that seemed to speak directly to our mission. Maybe we think we are ready, but we aren't.

Gary's talk took me back to 1995 when I wanted to lead a class at my church on the Great Books of the Christian Faith. I wanted to start with *Knowing God* by J. I. Packer. I even had a study guide, and I read and reread Packer's book during the summer, making notes in the margin, preparing to teach.

When I shared with Cyndi my dream of a Great Books class, she smiled sweetly the way she does to let me know she loves me and believes in me and is proud of me, and then she asked, "But who would come to a book class?"

Well, I wasn't sure who would come, but surely there would be a few people. I thought it was a great plan to read Augustine and Luther and Eusebius and Calvin, and discuss their approaches to Christianity, and together we'd all grow smarter about God and have a better understanding of how we should live. I thought it was a great and worthwhile project, and I was just the one to lead it.

About two weeks before my Knowing God class was scheduled to begin, after I'd made lots of notes and thought I was ready, the church asked me to teach something else instead. They had a video series about . . . I don't remember, but I think it was relating to one another as church members. They wanted me to teach that instead of the book. Bummer.

I mean, I was flattered to be asked to lead a class of the type normally led by one our staff ministers. I appreciated the confidence they had in me, and I knew I had the skills and heart to teach the material. But I also felt the loss of a dream, and I wondered if someone at my church thought I was too much of a lightweight to teach Packer, or thought *Knowing God* was the wrong book, and so on. Mostly I assumed the pastor didn't trust me.

The video study went well and was well attended, but it was like a lot of canned courses I've taught where an hour's worth of material gets stretched into a twelve-week course. Those classes get hard to teach toward the end, after everything has been said two or three ways.

I never mentioned my idea of a Great Books course after that (except to Cyndi). I no longer thought I was the guy to do it, if indeed it should be done.

Twelve years passed, and there I was at the men's weekend.

Gary Barkalow pulled out one of those huge Scottish swords and swung it around the stage and said, "This is a powerful and lethal weapon; but imagine going into battle with a sword this big before you've been trained to use it. You would hurt as many of your own men as the enemy. Having a powerful weapon from God can be dangerous if used before God makes you ready."

It occurred to me that for two and a half years, I had been leading a men's book study class on Thursday mornings. I was doing what I once dreamed of doing, only ten years later. I was fulfilling an old dream without even knowing it.

But the difference was way more than ten years. When I first wanted to teach a Great Books class, my goal was that we'd all become smarter in the ways of God; now my goal was that we'd grow together in our Christian walk, a band of brothers on a common mission. Ten years ago my focus was on books and intellect; now it was on men and community. I wasn't ready for that type of mission ten years ago—I needed more training.

When I first started hiking in the Guadalupe Mountains, my goal was to conquer the distance, learn the skills, and have a story to write. But through the years I've learned the value of hiking with my guys. And some of my best moments are after we are all down off the mountain and settled into our bus seats for the long drive back to Midland. The bus is soon filled with the buzz of telling stories and displaying scars, of sharing photos and joining hearts. That part of the trip always makes me happy. Hiking together turns friends into brothers, but I wonder if it isn't the bus ride home more than the trail itself that knits us together.

And so I also learned that the value of a great book goes beyond the information itself; it lies in our discussions. As we learn the book together, friends become brothers.

> **From everyone who has been given much, much will be demanded; and from the one who has been entrusted with much, much more will be asked.**
>
> **—Luke 12:48**

26

Entrusted to Me

The seminar leader was teaching from 1 Peter 5:2–4:

> Be shepherds of God's flock that is under your care, watching over
> them—not because you must, but because you are willing, as God
> wants you to be; not pursuing dishonest gain, but eager to serve;
> not lording it over those entrusted to you, but being examples to
> the flock. And when the Chief Shepherd appears, you will receive
> the crown of glory that will never fade away.

He asked, "Which words jump out at you?" People said "shepherds,"
"care," "willing," "serve," and "examples." But the word that grabbed
me was "entrusted."

God trusted me with a classroom of young couples and with a handful
of men. He trusted me to take care of them, to speak the truth to them, to
share my heart with them—more importantly, to share God's heart.

To entrust is to let someone take care of something for you because
you believe they will protect it. You might entrust a nursing home with the
care of your parents or entrust an accountant with your finances. If a friend
entrusts you with a secret, she trusts you not to tell anyone.

I love this notion that we have been entrusted with valuable things,
entrusted by God himself. It's as if God said to us, "Here, take care of this
for me for a while."

We are entrusted with individuals, with classes, with the trail itself, with
insight and knowledge. Being entrusted means not hiding but spreading

80

around and increasing. It means not worrying about big numbers or big markets or big classes but ministering to those with whom we've been entrusted.

Lately I have started using the phrase "catch and release" to describe how I want to teach. I've never been interested in building a huge class. I am a good teacher and I know a lot of people would benefit from being in our class, but I don't see numbers as the measure of success.

I want to catch and release people. I want them to join our class and learn and grow and develop lifelong practices that will draw them close to God, and then I want them to move on to find their own place of ministry. I am not trying to accumulate followers but release ministers.

27

New Assignment

Even hiking my favorite trails can get exhausting, and teaching is similar. After thirteen years of teaching adults my own age, I was worn out. I felt like this group had heard everything I had to say more than once, and I was simply marking time. Not only that, but Cyndi was part of our church media ministry, and she had quit coming to class, preferring instead to work in the media booth during the middle worship service, which met the same time as our class. Also, all the department leadership had moved on to other assignments, so I was left behind to do all the organizing as well as the teaching. I was exhausted, weary, lonely, and overworked. I was approaching complete burnout.

However, I didn't know how bad off I was until Mark Foster took me to lunch one day and said that when he had visited our class, it was obvious to him I was in need of a change. As soon as he said it, I realized it was true.

Too often we let church programs run on and on, never sensing when they get tired or worn out and need to be killed in favor of something fresh. I wonder if we ought to set a five- or ten-year sunset on everything we begin in order to stir the pot and promote new relationships and fresh teaching.

Mark asked if I would consider moving to a new class made of newly married young adults. The thought of such a big change was just frightening enough to be exciting. I told Mark I would talk it over with Cyndi, but I could already feel my loyalties shifting and my heart moving to a new work. Mark was marking a new trail for me, and I knew it was time for a change in direction.

It wasn't a simple consideration, though.

I was concerned about my teaching methods. I had read just enough about millennials versus baby boomers to know the worldview and learning style of this new, younger class would be different from mine. These youngsters wouldn't know who the Doobie Brothers were and wouldn't remember any Watergate conspiracy names. My cultural references would be out of date. Even worse, my cultural *understanding* might be dated.

I searched the Internet for information about teaching twenty-somethings—what they needed, what they feared, how they thought. I wanted to find new writers to influence my thinking. So far the most influential writers in my life had been Phillip Yancey, Charles Swindoll, and Henri Nouwen. I had devoured all the books from each of them, hoping they would inspire and inform my teaching. Who should I add to the mix now?

My search led me to the "emerging church." I loved reading about its return to ancient worship practices and a flexible understanding of serous doctrinal issues.

That research led me to Leonard Sweet, Brian McLaren, Rob Bell, Donald Miller. I know some of those names scare conservative believers because they get squishy on topics we consider firm and permanent, but for me, reading these fresh voices from my own thirty-years depth of Baptist life was fun.

The biggest influence during this phase of my life came by accident at a Promise Keepers meeting in Dallas with my son, Byron. I enjoy these giant gatherings because it's fun to be one of us where there are so many of us. But it is hard for me to relate directly to the speakers, most of whose backgrounds and presentation styles are foreign to me.

However, at this particular Promise Keepers, the opening speaker was a hipster-looking guy I had never heard of from Los Angeles named Erwin McManus. Before the weekend was over, I had bought two copies of two of his books, one pair for me and one pair for Byron. Since then I have read all of Erwin's books and listen to him regularly on podcast.

The two other dominant voices that came through to me from out of the crowd were Gary Barkalow and John Eldredge. These men have shaped my teaching style and focus more than anyone else.

When I look back at that summer of 2004 and how much I learned, how much I changed in getting ready for this new class, I realize the energy that comes through such change.

I was a tired teacher, equipped with good teaching chops but exhausted from the load and out of ideas. The change pushed me toward new influences I wouldn't have found otherwise, and it opened up my teaching and enlivened my life. I decided to never look at change with as much fear, ever again.

> *He said to them, "Therefore every teacher of the law who has become a disciple in the kingdom of heaven is like the owner of a house who brings out of his storeroom new treasures as well as old."*
>
> **—MATTHEW 13:52**

Part 5: High Alpine Meadow

There is something that happens to my heart when I have my feet on dirt, whether I'm walking or running or hiking. Covering ground, feeling the dirt, changes me. I want to chart my way on a topo map. I want to feel the changing angles in my legs. I want to experience the trail.

I've never longed to go car camping the same way I long to go backpacking, even though both would put me in nature. I don't have the same desire to simply set up camp and relax around a fire. Merely being in nature isn't what is important to me; I want to move in it. I want trail dirt on my shoes.

28

Our Responsibility

I was writing in Whataburger one morning when Dennis Perry came in and sat beside me. Dennis was a minister on staff at my church. He was eating a quick breakfast taquito on his way to the airport to fly to Orlando, Florida, for a weeklong Community Bible Study (CBS) meeting. He was deeply involved in the new CBS group, and he seemed to love that ministry.

Before he joined me, I had been reading a devotion on 1 Samuel 3:1–9, about the time God spoke to young Samuel in the night and Eli had to explain what was happening. The writer wrote, "Back in the past of his mind, Eli vaguely remembers that voice—a voice that needs to be identified as we respond to it . . . but Samuel has not heard this voice before."[38]

I wrote at the bottom of the page, "It is our responsibility as seasoned leaders to not forget the voice of God, and to help young Samuels know how to recognize God's voice when they hear it."

I thought it was ironic, or coincidental, or fortuitous that I should be thinking about Eli when Dennis showed up. I told him what I was writing about: that we older guys who have been following Jesus for a long time—we Elis—have an obligation to share with the young Samuels around us, guys who are on the edge of their lives and moving into the bigger world of God.

I don't want to end up as one of those old silverbacks who continually lean against the past. I get tired of stories about how good things used to be. I want to lean forward into the future. I have promises to keep.

—BERRY

29

A Reluctant Leader

In December, a minister at my church, Paul Byrom asked if I'd be part of a new men's ministry he was pulling together at our church. I said I would gladly be part of it, but I didn't think I should teach it or lead it. It seemed like I ended up as the guy standing in front of the room too often, and I worried that I was teaching too much and listening too little.

Another reason I was reluctant to lead a men's ministry was because I never considered myself a man's man. I was not an athlete, didn't play golf, only followed sports sporadically, would rather be by myself reading or writing than hanging with the men spitting and whittling, didn't hunt or even own a gun, rarely went fishing, had never been to drag races, and was totally indifferent about NASCAR.

But when Paul told me they were going to start by going through the *Wild at Heart* materials, I knew I was full in. I think Paul knew it too. My wife, Cyndi, had already tipped him off during one of their early morning runs. I had read the book twice in the past six months and had just returned from a Wild at Heart Boot Camp retreat in Buena Vista, Colorado. I was still vibrating from all I'd learned.

What happened next can be summed up by this quote from Mark Batterson's book, *Wild Goose Chase*: "Nothing is more unnerving or disorienting than passionately pursuing God. . . . He will take you places you never could have imagined going by paths you never knew existed."[39]

I was serving in city government at the time, and my weekly schedule was booked solid. When could I squeeze in a class? I told Paul my only opening was 6:30–7:30 a.m. Thursdays. He thought that might work. He said, "We'll try it and see if anyone shows up."

It was an immediate success; we had fifteen to twenty consistent attendees. I thought the class would wind down after we finished *Wild at Heart*, but the men wanted to keep going. What's our next book? They asked. I said, Give me a week to figure it out.

I had to scramble, look over my bookshelf, and start picking books to study.

And then, before I knew it, something I never expected: we celebrated ten years of that same men's ministry, which is now known as Iron Men. It has grown into a band of like-minded men dedicated to helping each other live solid, godly lives as leaders, husbands, and fathers. Through those ten years we've seen at least 150 men participate, many returning year after year.

Many of the greatest delights along the trail are the stories you never planned or imagined.

I doubt I would've agreed to be my group's leader if I'd known it would be a ten-year-plus commitment, and what a shame if I hadn't. The relationships I've formed during those ten years have been the most significant influence in my spiritual formation. I did not expect that.

The name of our group comes from Proverbs 27:17, which says, "As iron sharpens iron, so one person sharpens another." But sharpening each other isn't all we do. We also smooth each other. We're like old wooden-handled tools that show the wear of constant use, the smoothed portions worn by the hands that used them. Our constant contact with each other wears away the rough spots, leaving us with the pattern of our fellow valiant men. The older I get, the more I look forward to being worn smooth by these men.

And we don't just study books together. We do a lot of hiking in the nearby Guadalupe Mountains, taking at least two big trips each year. Why? Because men make friends outside, especially when they're doing something difficult together. One morning, on the strenuous opening mile of switchbacks of the Guadalupe Peak Trail, I mentioned to my friend Paul

Ross, "Surely there is an easier way to do ministry." Well, there might be, but easier isn't the same as better. I don't know any other way to duplicate the time I get to spend with my guys; the extended conversations along the trail are my favorite part of the trip.

I'm often surprised that the guys want to go up the same trail again—same mountain, same hike, year after year. But of course, we don't do it for the actual hiking; we do it for the time together on the trail. As William Blake wrote, "Great things are done when Men & Mountains meet / This is not Done by Jostling in the Street."[40] Lives are changed on the trail.

So many times we've come down off the trail, collapsed into our seats on the bus, changed into comfortable shoes, gulped water, scarfed down Advil, and immediately started telling stories from the day and congratulating each other. Before long we are discussing our most recent book study or Bible lesson, or we are asking advice. It makes me happy. My heart swells and my brain settles, proud to be one of us. The world is full of men who live their entire lives with no real friends who will hike to the top of the mountains with them, yet I have a bus full of guys like that.

> *For most men, physical movement, especially if difficult and challenging, brings us together in a way that sitting in a class together can never do. Men doing something hard together become brothers.*
>
> *—BERRY*

30

Fear of Speaking Out

One afternoon I drove to the high school track to run intervals. As I was warming up, I thought about what Cyndi had said to me Sunday evening after the church ministry fair. She asked if I thought it was funny or ironic that I was standing in front of the men's ministry table as a spokesman.

What Cyndi was asking didn't register until that afternoon when I walked out on the track. She was referring to my earlier surprise at my new role as a men's ministry leader. Cyndi wondered if I saw the irony that not only had I found a place as a teacher of men and developed a loyal following, but I had become a spokesman for the ministry without trying. Who knew that would happen?

As I ran an interval counting my steps and fighting through the ninety-five-degree August air, I wondered why I resisted this leadership position so much. I thought about the upcoming Boot Camp and the guys who were going with me and how nervous I felt to be "hosting" them. Why did it make me nervous?

I realized it was because, *What if the guys didn't have a good experience and thought it was lame and a waste of time and money and it was my fault for talking them into doing it and now they thought I was a lightweight leader and my ideas were trivial and my opinions should be discarded?*

As I continued to run, I realized how a particular fear had ruled much of my life. It was the fear of giving specific instruction or recommendations based on my own word. I was afraid people wouldn't like me or take me seriously if I was wrong. I have no problem saying, "Do this because the Bible says so," but I have a big problem saying, "Do this because I say so." In the same vein I realized how comfortable I was saying, "This book really helped me," but I felt uncomfortable saying, "This book will be good for you, read it."

If I say, "It was good for me," I cannot be wrong. No one can disagree. It is an irrefutable statement. But if I say, "It will be good for you," I am wide open to disagreement and criticism.

I had been captured by this fear. Where did it come from? What was the source? Why did it dominate my thinking? I realized how dangerous it was. My fear to speak out, make direct recommendations, and trust my own opinions was a direct hit on my calling from God. My gifts and purpose are about teaching and writing and speaking, about opening windows for people, and the fear of expressing my own opinions shut down those gifts. This was direct spiritual attack designed to sit me down and shut me up.

The first argument from fear is that you're not qualified.[41]

—**Jon Acuff**

31

Valiant Men

We only learn how to be effective trail markers by hiking the trails ourselves.

The story of Saul's becoming king is one of my favorite Bible stories because of the way God prepared Saul for leadership even after he took the job. I tend to ask God to prepare me for the next opportunity, give me the skills for my next ministry, so I will be ready when called. But as with Saul, most of my training has come after I've made the commitment to the new position, not before.

The Bible says Saul was told, "The Spirit of the Lord will come powerfully upon you . . . and you will by changed into a different person" (1 Sam. 10:6). The passage goes on to say, "Once these signs are fulfilled, do whatever your hand finds to do, for God is with you" (v. 7).

Wow, what a job assignment! Let the Spirit of God change you, then use your own judgment. It has become one of my most frequent prayers through the years: "God, change my heart." Sometimes he changes it from anger to love, sometimes from bitterness to acceptance, but often he changes it from timidity to courage.

My other favorite part of the Saul story takes place after Saul was officially crowned king. It says he went home "accompanied by valiant men whose hearts God had touched" (1 Sam. 10:26).

When Saul's story began, he was just a young man making his own way through the world on his own. Now he has guys. And not just ordinary guys but valiant men with godly hearts.

I recently went through the exercise of writing down the story of my own life, including all the people who have mentored me and influenced me. One of the biggest blessings was to consider the valiant men God has put in my life. I tend to think of myself as a loner, a hermit, until I tally the men who surround me. My life would be so dismal without them.

[Christ] demonstrated that you have not done anything until you have changed the lives of men.[42]

—HOWARD HENDRICKS

32

Journey Groups

My reluctant entrance into men's ministry eventually morphed into three parts: our Thursday morning book study, our twice-yearly hikes and occasional backpacking trips, and a mentoring program we called Journey Groups.

The idea for Journey Groups began when my friend John Witte came back from a retreat with young college-age men and realized how much they struggled making life decision. He developed a training program based on ideas laid out by Andy Stanley in his book *The Principle of the Path* about how to make good decisions.

I signed up to do a twelve-week session with John so I could learn how to lead them myself. I thought his Journey Group plan might be a good way to speak into the hearts of the young men God was bringing into my life.

Once I started, it occurred to me that the men in my group were a little older than John's college students, and while all of us struggle with making good decisions, decision making wasn't the deepest need for my guys. Also, it wasn't the message my heart wanted to teach. I never felt comfortable with it or thought I was adding much value to the men's lives.

Soon after starting the program, I attended a workshop in Breckinridge, Colorado, led by Gary Barkalow of Noble Heart Ministries. One afternoon, listening to one of the guys talk through exercises that revealed his passions and, ultimately, his calling from God, and it all became clear. This was the direction I need to take Journey Group in. Uncovering the calling

God gave us was much more the message of my heart than decision making, or recovery, or anything else.

When I got home I reworked the materials for Journey Group and recruited two friends who had already gone through the program with John to help me try out the new plan.

We meet as a group of three guys for ten sessions, usually in a local restaurant. We need at least an hour and a half together. Here is the schedule:

Weeks 1, 2, 3: Each man tells his story in turn, one story each week. We want to hear the story of a man's life, not just a five-minute testimony. The leader goes first to establish the pattern.

Weeks 4, 5, 6: Each man discusses his Myers-Briggs test results. If our story tells how we grew up (the *nurture* aspect of our life), this personality survey shows our individual behavioral tendencies (the *nature* aspect of our life). This usually results in more stories, but this time the stories are about relationships rather than events.

Weeks 7, 8, 9: Each man goes over results from exercises designed to uncover our dreams and passions, gifts from God that often get covered up and hidden by the daily debris of life.

Week 10: Each man hears feedback from the other two men.

This last session is the heart of Journey Group. Each of us makes comments about the other guys, based on our notes. We can talk about whatever we want, but the specific aim will be our observations of each guy's journey (life story, victories, defeats, tendencies, successes, dangers, etc.) and each guy's glory (the weight of his life, the effect of his life, where he should step up). I record this session on a digital recorder because it is too much data to remember. The recording allows the men to listen and digest at their leisure.

In today's world we seldom have another man who knows our story look us in the eyes and give real advice. It is a powerful moment. Guys in particular seem to always think they are alone or that their struggles are unique. To know that other guys are fighting, struggling, and working through similar challenges is valuable. It gives courage to keep fighting.

I don't have an agenda when we start a Journey Group except for the process. I let the process run and see where it goes. The fact that it has always gone well speaks to the value of the program and to the value of showing up and being myself with other men.

A trail never explains itself and doesn't tell where it leads. It simply invites to follow.

Every time I come home and tell Cyndi how amazed I am that it still works, she just smiles. She understands it better than I do.

"For what I received I passed on to you" (1 Cor. 15:3).

This has become a life verse for me, and with each passing year I feel the obligation more strongly. I realize anew how blessed I was with a deep spiritual foundation and broad reach. When I was younger I took all that for granted, but as I get older I see it as an obligation. I must give away —give back—what was passed on to me.

And another thing: I believe spiritual knowledge and insight needs room to breathe. If I am not continually giving away, I can't expect to learn more myself. We are not deep wells of knowledge storing what we've learned, but pipelines that continually give away and receive anew. Not to give away is to stagnate.

—BERRY

Part 6: Gentle Descent

Hiking down from a mountaintop always takes longer than I think it should. I expect to move much faster, and I do, but never as fast as I'd hoped. However, walking downhill is certainly much easier than hiking uphill.

33

Standing Alone

As far back as I have memories I've longed for a life that mattered, a significant life. At first I thought it would derive from what I learned or accumulated. Later I assumed it would come from what I said or wrote. And now I realize that a life of significance comes not from transmitting facts or accumulating stuff but from lasting relationships. It comes from giving yourself away.

One June morning in 2013 I was sitting on the porch at Sam Williamson's house outside of Ann Arbor, Michigan, listening to the birds and breathing in the cool, damp early morning air. The world around me was deeper, greener, and richer than it was this time of year back home in Texas, which was still suffering from drought, and it opened my heart to listen.

I was there for a weekend workshop hosted by The Noble Heart ministries, designed to help us know and understand our calling from God. Our assignment for this morning was to write down our best understanding of that calling and try to reduce it to a manageable number of words, thus gaining a better vision of how to live our lives and choose our activities going forward.

I began by asking these questions: What are the things I absolutely have to do? What is most important for me to teach or write? Some possible answers:

Give away what I've received.

Inspire people to seek God with a focused effort.

Use my character and personality to change the world around me.

Live publicly, openly, vulnerably, transparently, honestly, and authentically.

Give myself away—my time, talents, energy, and focus.

Write essays and books that will set people free.

Bring order out of chaos—not in management or structure but in ideas.

Love the people God has entrusted to me.

I'd recently listened to an audio book titled, *Man Seeks God*, by Eric Weiner, and I thought his title described my life, the Man who seeks God, the Pilgrim for Christ. But that morning, all at once, I realized that simply seeking God would never be enough. I had to share what I found. And actually, even sharing was not enough; I had to bring people with me. My heart's desire was not to be just a pilgrim but a guide. I didn't want to journey alone.

I wrote in my journal, "I don't want to be the man who finds God standing alone."

It was the most truthful, close-to-my-own-heart statement I had made all weekend, so true that I was overwhelmed. I had to leave Sam's porch and walk down the road for a hundred yards to catch my breath. What did my heart really want to do? It wanted not merely to seek God for myself but to lead other people to a deeper life with God. A significant life could no longer be a pilgrim life; it had to become a trail-guide life. A life dedicated and committed to leading people to a deeper life with Christ.

I remember standing at the Pine Top campground in the Guadalupe Mountains one morning, watching the sun rise, and saying aloud, "I can't keep doing this by myself."

—BERRY

34

Learning to Surf

It was Wednesday morning in Kauai, and Cyndi and I drove to Kapaa (as in the movie *Honeymoon in Vegas*) to Kealia Beach to meet our old friend, Nephi, for surfing lessons. His company, named, simply enough, Learn to Surf, was featured in *The Ultimate Kauai Guide Book* which we used to make almost all our vacation decisions.

Afterward, Cyndi and I talked about Nephi. We took lessons from him on our last visit, and it was no accident that we called him again for this trip. I scribbled a list of things that made him a good teacher and role model.

First, Nephi gave just enough detail to get you started, but not enough to confuse you. Too often we teachers talk too much. We think we have to tell more than we actually do. I remember taking six guys to a Wild at Heart Boot Camp in 2006, and forcing myself to keep my mouth shut. I had already attended Boot Camp twice, and my tendency was to lead my friends by giving advice about the cool parts.

But they deserved the chance to learn their own lessons and have their own breakthroughs. They didn't need me to hold their hands. I had to continually remind myself to leave them alone and let them find what they needed instead of adding my own teaching on top of what the Boot Camp speakers were saying. This was especially hard since my son and son-in-law were among the group, and I had a lot invested in those two relationships.

We teachers need to learn how little we can share and yet still keep the lesson focused on the right things. Nephi did that. He gave just enough instruction to move us to the next step.

The first thing he taught us was how to pull the surfboard tail first into the ocean with both hands so the waves wouldn't turn us around as we walked out into the surf. Then he showed us how to lie down on the board and get up to our feet. He led everyone through a few practice rounds there on the beach before taking us out into the water. Any more detail would have been too much to remember and probably made the experience even scarier.

Also, Nephi didn't feel the need to pump us up, as in, "Are you ready to surf big today?" "Who's feeling brave?" "Are there any big-wave surfers around here?" None of that. Personally, I don't enjoy exercise classes when the instructor keeps trying to pump me up. I've already decided to come to the class, so I don't need additional motivation. I often think the boisterous instructor is hoping we will holler back and make a lot of noise merely to satisfy his own ego.

Instead, Nephi was calm and knowledgeable. We simply wanted to trust him. He sounded like he had done this many times before, like he knew how to help, and that he genuinely wanted everyone to get up on their boards and have a great experience surfing.

Another thing: even though some of us beginning surfers weren't as young or as fit or as flexible or strong as the others, Nephi never even hinted, "Oh, you are going to have a tough time," or, "I'm not sure if you'll be able to do this." He taught the class *flat*, with the same positive expectations for everyone.

Not only that, but he had reasonable expectations. First, learn to stand up on the board; after that, we'll see how it goes. For those of us who took longer to catch on, he offered alternative moves, easier steps for getting up and standing on the board.

Finally, rather than scolding us for mistakes ("You are too far back!"), he made positive suggestions like "Try moving a little forward and see what happens." As a result, we never felt like we were doing it wrong, only that we needed a little fine-tuning.

Like most fun activities, surfing comes with its own risk. Cyndi's board flipped on her first run and busted her lip. Of course she didn't stop surfing. She kept going and going, even though she was bleeding. Nephi said, "They don't get any tougher than her."

> *When you have a guide you can trust, you don't need to worry about what's on the path ahead.*[43]
>
> **—BOB GOFF**

35

Elijah and Elisha

God played a joke on us Christians by anointing two powerful prophets back-to-back who had almost the same name and performed some of the same miracles. I got these two confused until I realized they served God in alphabetical order: Elijah, then Elisha. Of course they didn't speak English, and the alphabetical order thing may not hold up in Hebrew, but it helps me anyway.

Elisha was a student of Elijah's. Elijah, toward the end of his life, knew his time was winding down, so he made a tour around the country checking in on other prophets, and Elisha went with him.

Second Kings chapter 2 chronicles Elijah's farewell tour. At every stop, he tried to talk Elisha into staying behind. I don't know if Elijah wanted to walk those last steps alone or if he was giving Elisha a face-saving way to drift away. Maybe Elijah was trying to talk Elisha out of accompanying him to check his resolve: How bad do you want to come?

Elijah said, "Stay here; the Lord has sent me to Bethel."

Elisha replied, "As surely as the Lord lives and as you live, I will not leave you."

This same conversation occurred several times. It reminded me of what Sam Gamgee said to Frodo Baggins in the movie *The Fellowship of the Ring*: "I made a promise, Mr. Frodo. A promise. 'Don't you leave him Samwise Gamgee.' And I don't mean to. I don't mean to."

Later Frodo said, "Go back, Sam. I'm going to Mordor alone."

Sam said, "Of course you are. And I'm coming with you."[44]

I think Elisha knew he had a loyal follower in Elisha, but maybe it was hard to believe. He'd spent most of his prophet career alone, often lonely, and it probably didn't even seem real that someone would want to follow him all the way out to the edge of his life. Also, even though he sensed the end was near, he didn't know how it would happen. He didn't want Elisha to commit to the unknown.

Elisha was having none of it. He wanted to stay with Elijah to the very end, and he longed for a touch from God. He wanted to be like Elijah. He said, "Let me inherit a double portion of your spirit."

Elijah replied that whether or not that happened was up to God, not him. He couldn't pick his own successor, only God could do that, even if they almost had the same name. Elijah knew it wasn't his gift to give.

It sounds a little arrogant for Elisha to say, I want twice what you have, but I doubt he meant it that way. I think he was paying honor to Elijah, saying he understood the most important and valuable part of Elijah's life, and he wanted some of that. No, he wanted *all* of that, a double portion.

Can you understand Elisha's desire to have double the spirit of his teacher? He wasn't being arrogant or presumptuous. He wasn't asking for double the number of miracles, double fame, or double influence. Think of the people who have influenced you most. Wouldn't you want God to give you a double portion of their spirit, their motivation, their passion, and their heart?

When we invest in the lives of other people, we transmit not only what we know, but more importantly what we are.[45]

—WALTER HENRICHSEN

36

Not Losing Heart

The Tejas Trail in the Guadalupe Mountains is a long four-mile climb, a constant grade with very few switchbacks. It just keeps climbing and climbing and climbing. Much of the trail has been blasted into the solid limestone mountain, and the surface is rough and covered with rocks.

My first time to hike Tejas was in drizzling rain. More than once I came around a promontory and the fog was so thick I couldn't see down the mountain behind me or down the slope beside me. All I could see clearly was one turn above me and one turn below me. The sensation was eerie. I couldn't tell how high I'd climbed or how much farther I had to go. I felt like I was climbing in a dream world—or pacing on a mountain treadmill.

I finally sat down on a big, flat rock, took off my backpack, and pulled out my rain jacket and hat. It hadn't been cold enough down at the bottom of the mountain to need the jacket, but I knew if my shirt got soaked from the damp air, I would be miserable when I got to the top. I decided to suit up before going any further.

As I hiked, I kept stepping in water running down the trail. Not a good sign. Water seldom runs anywhere in the Guadalupes, so seeing water on the trail meant the rain was coming down even harder up higher, and I was just seeing part of the runoff. Not only that but the higher I climbed, the more the temperature dropped, and the wet ground alongside the trail soon became dusted with snow. Eventually, snow began to cover the trail, and the low spots in the trail were often filled with cold slushy water. I was nervous about pitching my tent on top of snow, and I kept checking my watch to calculate when I would have enough daylight to turn around and hike back down to my car before dark if it came to that.

Therefore we do not lose heart. Though outwardly we are wasting away, yet inwardly we are being renewed day by day.

—*2 Corinthians 4:16*

My friend James Mims was once asked about the loss of his wife after sixty years of marriage. James said he was grateful every day for the time they had together, and then he added this bit of advice: "Keep your eyes on the doughnut, not the hole."

This is not a passive way of living. Choosing not to lose heart requires diligence and focus. Satan wants nothing more than to drag us into despair and hopelessness, taking us out of the battle.

About a year ago I was at a men's retreat where we talked about our calling and fleshed out some plans for moving forward and fulfilling our passions. One man had great ideas about a vacation house he was building in Idaho, and how he could bring people in to help him with the construction and use the time for mentoring and building truth into their lives. Not only did he have a great idea and a passion to make it work, but it was energizing to hear him describe it. We all joined in with suggestions to help round out his idea. It was a great time.

But the very next morning, when we shared our takeaway with the larger group, this man was a completely different person. His head was low, his spirit beaten down, and his talk was, essentially, "I don't know what I was thinking. It won't work. Now I'm lost and don't know what to do next."

We were stunned. It was shocking to see someone so full of hope get taken down by the enemy so quickly and completely. I had never seen anything like it. Living in hope requires constant attention. We have to defend against attack at every moment.

*Guard the good deposit that was entrusted to you—
guard it with the help of the Holy Spirit who lives in us.*

—2 TIMOTHY 1:14

37

Sharing Our Lives

Being an example is hard. How many famous people insist they are not role models because they don't want to defend the way they live. It takes courage to stand up as an example, but the apostle Paul told his young student Timothy to be exactly that—an example: "Don't let anyone look down on you because you are young, but set an example for the believers in speech, in conduct, in love, in faith and in purity" (1 Tim. 4:12).

Gordon MacDonald writes that the literal rendering of Paul's words, "Set an example," is "Stamp yourself on people's lives."[46]

Stamp yourself on people's lives. That is even bigger and bolder than setting an example. It is an intentional move to change the way others live through the weight of your own life. Being an example is brave but passive. Stamping yourself is intentional and active.

It took me over forty years to understand that I couldn't change the world as a hermit. I spent too many years running away from people. They made me uncomfortable, and I just didn't want to bother being sociable. I was content to stay in my cave and read and write, coming out only occasionally to teach a class before retreating back inside. But one day it occurred to me that a hermit has very little impact on the people around him, regardless of his writing skills or teaching insights. People's lives are changed when they let someone live close to them, and I couldn't be an agent of change unless I became one of those who got close.

Even after teaching adults for ten years or more, I was more comfortable being known and admired as a good teacher (what I did) than as a good man (who I was). I avoided setting myself as an example, and becoming comfortable with that has come slowly. I'm still not so sure I have anything to offer that a thousand other men don't have, but I have stopped resisting. Instead I've learned to embrace what my calling requires of me; I have reversed course, and now I work to pull people in close to me. Closer is better.

Paul's notion of Timothy's influence was sweeping. He wanted Timothy to live the sort of life others could study and analyze and emulate . . .

In speech (the things a person says and the way he says them)

In life (the qualities of one's living routine)

In love (the characteristics of one's personal relationships)

In faith (the way a man or woman loves God)

In purity (one's moral life)

To live like that requires constant attention. I used to think it required hard discipline and rigid spiritual practices, and maybe it does, but that line of thinking reveals how I assumed it was all up to me and my perfect performance. No wonder I avoided it. Now I understand it is less about discipline and more about surrender—as in Psalm 139:23: "Search me, God, and know my heart; test me and know my anxious thoughts."

Now I pray, "Show me how to live to draw me toward you, and show me what to say and write that draws others close to you." Not that I am so noble, but I've released trying to perfect myself. No one wants to follow a perfectionist, anyway.

Ten years ago my focus was on books and intellect; today it is on men and community.

—BERRY

38

Skill and Willingness

Reading one morning in my *Daily Bible* from Exodus 35 about the construction of the temple in the wilderness, I noticed a connection between the words *skill* and *willing*. Over and over, the commands from God began with "Everyone who is willing" and "All who are skilled." I counted fourteen times in chapter 35 where one or the other word was used. I don't think we can ignore the connection.

Willingness is motivation caused by God's moving in our heart. We can teach ourselves to be willing just like we can learn to be grateful or generous. God is already pulling us in that direction, and all we have to do is go along, practice willingness until it becomes part of our identity.

But the story in Exodus also calls for skill. Too often we assume everyone else has skills but we don't. We tend to downplay our own skills and overplay everyone else's. In general most of us are terrible at judging our own best qualities, which is why we need close friends to point them out. We need someone to remind us, "You are good at that," or "You shine when you talk about that," or "When you do that, people sit up and listen and follow you."

We have skills, and when we willingly use them, a place for God gets built.

We often confuse genius with mastery. Genius is a gift we are given; mastery is the stewardship of our gifts.[47]

—ERWIN MCMANUS

113

39

A Simple Journey

My journey began when I read this quote from Yvon Chouinard, founder of Patagonia: "The more you know, the less you need."[48] I was hooked. I want to know more and I want to need less.

This is the backpacker's dilemma. Every ounce we carry makes the trip more enjoyable, more comfortable, and safer. And yet every ounce we carry also makes our trip less possible, less enjoyable, less comfortable, and less safe. The more things we are afraid of, the more gear we carry and the heavier our pack becomes.

After every backpacking trip, I pull out my gear list and mark the items I actually used and make notes for next time, the goal being to whittle away the list to minimize my load. I'm trying to use my experience in order to need less. "The more you know, the less your need."

Then a new friend added this: "Risk increases as one's range of options decreases."

So the formula was more complicated than I thought. Having less and living more simply wasn't necessarily easier. In fact, it reduced the range of options, which meant taking on more risk.

I asked my Facebook friends, "Is Chouinard's quote—'The more you know, the less you need'—true for life in general, or just backpacking?" Here are some of the answers I received:

"I think it is true in general. I find life being simpler and simpler as I go through it. I just find I need less."

"It takes a huge spiritual discipline to be simple."

"As I age, my need for things, the stuff I own and think I need, is changing."

"Graceful aging means continually throwing the excess over the side; constant winnowing."

A few days later, I read this in my *Daily Bible*, from Psalm 116:6: "The Lord protects the simplehearted."

That's cool. Not simpleminded or purehearted, which are more common words, but simplehearted. I asked my Facebook friends another question: What do you think it means to be simplehearted?:

"One whose emotional needs are easily met."

"Someone who doesn't seek to complicate things."

"One who loves first, last, and always."

"Integrity of heart."

"A heart that is uncomplicated and less cluttered by life stuff."

"Unmixed motives."

"Being fully alive and optimal." (I really liked the word "optimal.")

I didn't stop there. My mind was now locked onto the idea of simplicity when I read this from Peter Matthiessen's *The Snow Leopard*: "The sense of having one's life needs at hand, of traveling light, brings with it intense energy and exhilaration. Simplicity is the whole secret of well-being."[49] I want to live more simply, both in regard to how much stuff I need (less and less), and in regard to my heart (uncluttered and full of integrity).

Merely having less isn't enough, though. Nobody wants to live a stripped-down, lowest-bidder life. We need something deeper. We need meaning. John Maeda, in his book *The Laws of Simplicity*, wrote, "Simplicity is about subtracting the obvious and adding the meaningful."[50]

What do *you* do to simplify your life? Does it add meaning?

At some point, nearly every backpacker will wonder: How can I lighten my load? . . . The goal of any ultralight makeover: pack smarter to feel lighter, go farther, see more. The rewards, we believe, are worth the effort.[51]

—REI

Part 7: Next Trail

At the Chamisa Trail trailhead near Santa Fe, New Mexico, I noticed two mostly parallel trails with a sign reading, "Alternate Route More Difficult." I decided the alternate route was the one for me. Not to make the hike harder, but to make the experience more significant.

I thought about how many times I've driven across town to a potentially contentious church council meeting or another late night mentoring session, or chewed over a Bible lesson I was supposed to teach in two days, and found myself wondering what it would be like to live a simpler life.

One time on the Guadalupe Peak Trail, just as we finished the opening switchbacks and stopped to drink some water, my friend and guide Paul Ross said, "There must be an easier way to do ministry." We both nodded in agreement, even though we both knew neither of us would be satisfied following that easier way.

I spent years watching my parents live lives fully engaged with other people, giving away their talents and energy, choosing the Alternate Route More Difficult. And now, following that family tradition, I feel a deep-heart calling to help people live deeper lives with God. Even as I long for a simpler life, I know I'll never be happy if I'm not engaged with the alternate route.

The alternate route, the more difficult route, the meaningful route, calls out to us. Following our calling is never the easier trail.

40

What We Leave Behind

I knew this moment would finally come, and yet it still gave me pause when it happened. I was working as a contract engineer for Apache Corporation, sitting in my own cubicle at my own desk minding my own business, looking through an old file, trying to reconstruct the history of the wellbore, when I turned a page and saw my own name. It was on a recommendation to repair a casing leak, and I had written it in April 1988, twenty-three years and eight employers ago. Fortunately it was for a necessary repair that turned out to be successful, not some farfetched recommendation I made in my youth that embarrasses me now. That day may yet come.

I was reminded of a line from the 2003 Tim Burton movie *Big Fish*: "Fate has a way of circling back on a man; things look different than they did at a younger time of life."

I'm used to seeing my own work from long ago, but it's usually on my own shelves in my own home. I have handwritten running logs dating as far back as 1978 and journals from 1983. But this bit of writing was different. It was in someone else's file, a file that had been passed along from one operator to the next to the next, saved for all time and for countless engineers to read and pass judgment on. Or, I can only hope, to read and learn something.

I sent a photo of the recommendation with my signature to my friend Mark Foster, and he wrote back, "That's great stuff right there. It's so cool that you not only got a good gig with a good company but also a reminder of the footprints we leave." Well said by a fine man.

I think often about leaving footprints. About legacy. About lasting impact. Not that I care to be famous (I love my privacy too much), or even remembered (although I hope people will read and remember my books), but because I hope to leave a wake behind me of changed lives, who will pass on what I learned from faithful believers who invested their lives and energy into me.

There is a Bible verse I learned in college that still calls out my name: "The things which you have heard me say in the presence of many witnesses entrust to faithful people who will also be qualified to teach others" (2 Tim. 2:2). I am well aware of the wisdom that has been entrusted to me by godly men and women through the years. It makes me want to sit up straight and show respect. It makes me want to give it all away, entrust it to others.

I tweeted, "Enjoying my reengagement with engineering; but it reminds me that I want to leave behind more than old reports in old files."

Every time I read one of the apostle Paul's letters in the New Testament, I wonder if Paul had any sense that we would be reading his writing so many generations later. I doubt he imagined anything happening two thousand years after his death, but still, his writing rings with a timelessness of someone aware of his lasting impact. Yet he clearly wrote to address immediate concerns in a way that made sense to his contemporary readers. Paul invested in them— and in us.

I'm a little nervous to look too closely into more well files, but also excited to see if any of my old recommendations were ever completed. However, no matter what those files contain, it is the large circle of people God has allowed around me that reminds me what really matters. Not old, dried-up engineering recommendations but each other. The footprints I hope to leave are the ones right beside yours.

Don't confuse your resume with your legacy.[52]

—MARK SANBORN

41

Give It Away

The story bothered me for twenty-two miles. It was Sunday afternoon and I was cycling, taking advantage of an unseasonably warm winter day. I couldn't stop thinking about the parable used by our preacher that morning.

The parable of the bags of gold begins like this:

> "[The kingdom of heaven] will be like a man going on a journey, who called his servants and entrusted his wealth to them. To one he gave five bags of gold, to another two bags, and to another one bag, each according to his ability. Then he went on his journey. The man who had received five bags of gold went at once and put his money to work and gained five bags more. So also, the one with two bags of gold gained two more. But the man who had received one bag went off, dug a hole in the ground and hid his master's money." (Matt. 25:14–17)

According to the text, when the master returned, he asked what his servants had done with his wealth. The story goes well for the first two men who invested their shares and multiplied their value, but not for the third servant, who said, "I was afraid and went out and hid your gold in the ground" (v. 25).

The servant thought he was doing the right thing by hiding his master's wealth, but instead he wasted his opportunity to make the wealth grow.

121

The surprising part of the story, the part that sat on my mind for twenty-two miles, is what the master said to the third servant: "You wicked, lazy servant! . . . You should have put my money on deposit with the bankers, so that when I returned I would have received it back with interest. . . . Throw that worthless servant outside, into the darkness, where there will be weeping and gnashing of teeth" (vv. 26–27, 30).

Really? Throw him into darkness? He was just being cautious, protecting assets, cutting losses, and like that. Why was his punishment so harsh?

Well, the thing about this story is, it wasn't about the money. Jesus's stories were never about the value of money but about the condition of his listeners' hearts. The third man acted out of fear. He was afraid to take a risk with the gold because he didn't trust the heart of his master. He protected what he had by burying it and eventually lost it all.

Here are a couple of things I thought while riding my bike. First, God doesn't call us to live in fear but, rather, in power, love, and discipline. Second, we're accountable to God for what has been entrusted to us; we're accountable for the use of his resources, and he expects us to invest them rather than bury them.

I also thought of another Bible passage that has become important to me, from 2 Timothy 1:14: "Guard the good deposit that was entrusted to you."

What has God given to you? What does he want you, like the three men in Jesus's parable, to invest and multiply? How do you guard your most important things? (Hint: Your most prized gift from God isn't money.)

For me, the way to guard what God has given is to give it away. My most valuable possession from God is the truth and wisdom invested into me by my family and by other godly people for the past fifty years, and it is my obligation to give it all away. Not bury it for another book, not keep it hidden because I am afraid of what someone will say, not save it for a larger crowd, but invest it in the lives God has entrusted to me. To guard that good deposit, I have to give it away every day.

Author Annie Dillard described this need to give our life away in her book *The Writing Life*: "The impulse to keep to yourself what you have learned is not only shameful, it is destructive. Anything you do not give freely and abundantly becomes lost to you. You open your safe and find ashes."[53]

We don't become rich in God by accumulating but by giving away. We don't guard what God has given us by keeping quiet but by giving away. We have to invest what has been given to us in other people. If we don't, those very people God brought close to us will suffer. And so will we.

You and I are responsible for what we do with the lives God has given us by his grace.[54]

—JIM DENISON

42

Ten Years Blessed

One of our go-to movies, *The Bourne Supremacy*, has a heartbreaking scene in which Jason Bourne burns all the evidence of his girlfriend and their life together. He was making it harder for the bad guys to find him again. He wanted to disappear.

I've watched this scene so many times, and I always thought it sad that he had to destroy everything. For most of us, our most cherished possessions are the photos and stories of our lives.

What Jason Bourne was doing is the opposite of how I want to live. I want to leave lots of traces. I want to leave lots of evidence. I want to use the stories of my life to tell what God has given me.

Are you willing to build a trail?[55]

—*SETH GODIN*

43

Trail Guide

Our role as trail guides is to bring men to the window and pull back the curtain. One of my favorite comments about Rich Mullins was something I heard on a Christian radio talk show after Rich's death. A musician wondered what window Rich was looking out of. In other words, how did Rich Mullins see God when everyone else saw scenery? How was he able to see so much more?

Our job is to be a view finder, to offer both expanded and focused vision. To open up the bigger picture and show men that there's more to this life. To keep them moving past the early switchbacks that send casual hikers back to their cars prematurely; to reassure them, "It won't always be like this. It will eventually flatten out and the view will change. There's more to enjoy just around the corner. Let's go together."

Come and hear, all you who fear God; let me tell you what he has done for me.

—Psalm 66:16

44

Don't Measure Too Soon

I served as an elected official in city government for twelve years. When I left I was worried that I wouldn't have worth in the eyes of people. Worried that they wouldn't have a reason to listen to me, that I would lose the weight of my life. I knew I was a big fish in a small pond, but it was the pond I lived in, the pond I was trying to influence and change, the pond of my ministry.

But the true story is, after my last meeting, I never thought about any of that again. Either God removed that concern from me, or my mind changed focus so that it wasn't important. I don't know how it stopped bothering me, but it was gone like magic. It was *gone*. Government began to feel like my old life, long ago in fuzzy memory. Government went on without me, and good riddance.

Mike Foster wrote, in *Gracenomics*, "Don't make the mistake of measuring the value and contribution of your life too soon."[56] Why did I think my season of influence was over? Because I had been doing exactly what Mike Foster warned against.

I used to think my biggest contribution would be books, and maybe it will be still, but who knows. I may never touch more than a few hundred people. Now I look at my life and I think that Journey Groups and Iron Men and Compass may be the most important and biggest contributions of my life. But again, who knows. It is still too soon to tell.

I've settled with the idea I am not a good judge of my own value and contribution and never will be. So I should just keep pursuing the missions God puts in front of me. Just keep pushing. That's all, and that's enough.

After I turned fifty, my voice began to change, as older voices will. I recrafted my singing style and looked for new ways to tell a story with the voice I had.[57]

—**LINDA RONSTADT**

Part 8: Trail's End

Anyone who pays the price to hike to the top of a mountain sees something most other people never get to see. You have to carry the gear you need, hiking the hard trail with the heavy pack. You have to train yourself, take some risks, read the map, and follow the advice of other people in order to experience the summit.

I guess that's also true in all of life. It's certainly true in relationships: if you want to get to the high country, you have to pay the price, follow the advice of people, and do the hard training. But it is worth the effort. You get to travel where few people go. You get to experience the scenery from the top of the mountain instead of the desert floor. You get to see the world from the perspective of being loved in a deep relationship.

If you aren't willing to do that, you might spend your entire life down in the parking lot in the heat, hoping for shade and buying Cokes out of the vending machine. Maybe that's OK, but it isn't the best. Whether talking about relationships, or music, or spiritual growth, or a hobby, or worship, or teaching, or careers, if you want to see the high country, you have to hike the trail, do the hard work, learn the skills, and follow the advice.

What We Need

It's hard to know how much stuff to take and how much to leave behind. One Saturday morning the Iron Men were hiking Guadalupe Peak on the same day as the Junior High students from Wall, Texas. It was cold in the parking lot, and all those kids left the trailhead wearing too many layers of clothes. Our group started out a few minutes behind them, and as soon as the trail began to gain elevation, we noticed the bushes covered with fleeces and sweatshirts and jackets and hoodies where the kids had pulled them off because they got too hot. The trail had quickly revealed unneeded clothes and gear. And those kids started peeling and dumping.

In her book *Packing Light*, about a cross-country road trip, Allison Vesterfelt wrote, "Part of what makes it hard to pack light is that often you think you're already doing it."[58]

I've made a dozen or so backpacking trips during the last few years, and every trip I'm striving to pack lighter. In fact, my loaded backpack weighs fifteen pounds less than it did when I took up hiking. I've learned to leave stuff behind that I know I won't need or can suffer without until I get back down.

But Vesterfelt wasn't writing about backpacking, or even car-tripping. She was asking how to live her life with less baggage.

One of her friends asked, "How do you know when you're packing too light? . . . You don't want to leave your toothbrush behind. How do you decide what's your toothbrush and what's an extraneous pair of shoes?"[59]

Which brings me to one of my biggest question nowadays as I consider the next phase of my life: What should I carry along and what should I leave behind? What is extra, and what is essential for the trail ahead?

There are a lot of important things for us to do with our lives, but I am thinking of two big ones that seem more and more important the older I get.

We need to have someone who is speaking wisdom into our lives. And I don't think it will be a peer, or friend, or spouse. I think it needs to be someone who is further down the road than we are. I don't know if it has to be a personal contact, like a mentoring relationship, but I expect those are best. It might be a particular preacher or teacher whom we may never meet. It requires intentionality on our part: we have to choose to put ourselves under someone else's wisdom, or at least under the influence of their voice. It is a concern of mine at this time in my life that I don't have a personal contact or a mentor. I am continually asking the question, Who is speaking wisdom to me? I have some people I listen to on a regular basis; maybe that's my answer for now.

Another thing: We all need a place to give ourselves away. I don't mean giving money away, although I believe in that too. I mean, we need someplace where we are giving away our personality, our talents, our gifts to other people. Maybe as a musician, or a teacher, or a servant, or as part of a large movement. If we don't do this, we start to think the world is all about us and our own problems, and before long we find ourselves living tiny lives in tiny pictures with tiny hopes and dreams and tiny visions. We think we are living large, but we are fooling ourselves.

> **I just don't want to come to the end of my live and have to say, "I was gonna be different but I chickened out when I had the chance."[60]**
>
> **—GRACE**

46

What Do I Expect?

I don't expect to have a booming ministry full of guys I've discipled and guided. What I expect to happen—the way I expect God to bless what I am doing, bless what he is doing while I stand up in front of a group—is this: Guys will be attracted to me and want to become a part of what I'm doing. And a few of those guys will want even more; they will not only grasp the truths I have to share but embrace their own role and step into it. Those guys will be the ones who create the giant wake I long for: a long line of men following God who come from those few in my group.

However, I won't know who those guys are. I may never know who they are. They might not feel free to step up until I am out of the picture. So I teach them all, bring them all in, consider each of them to be one of "my guys," and let God be the one who taps them on the shoulder. Some of them will end up being heroes of the faith

So too with my writing blogs and books. I will keep doing it, sharing my heart, sharing my insights, trying to increase my readership and scope of influence, knowing that I may never be a bestselling author but also knowing that somewhere out there, someone will read something I've written, resonate with it, and run with it.

My job, in ministry and in writing, is to light lots of fuses, share lots of stories, inspire lots of heroes. I want to be Bagger Vance, Yoda . . . but I may never see or know my own Rannulph Junuh or Luke Skywalker. With this book, I am writing to some Rannulph Junah out there who probably doesn't yet know who he is or recognize his calling and potential. Maybe that's you. I hope, as you've meandered through this book, that some of its trail dust has stuck with you—a thought you can keep, an encouragement to keep you going, a vision that will capture your heart and make you, in turn, a trail marker for those who follow.

> *Your goal is to see a band of people raised up who have a strong, regular, personal intake of the Word of God and who have an effective prayer life. There are people who are living in vital union with Jesus Christ on a day-by-day basis, and through whose lives the life of Christ is flowing out in redemptive power to others around them.*"[61]
>
> —*LEROY EIMS*

Notes

1. *Pathways to Trail Building*, Bob Richards, ed., Tennessee Department of Environment and Conservation, http://atfiles.org/files/pdf/TNpathways.pdf, 4.

2. Woody Hesselbarth and Brian Vachowski, *Trail Construction and Maintenance Notebook*, 2004 ed., USDA Forest Service, quoted in Robert C. Berkby, *Lightly on the Land: The SCA Trail Building and Maintenance Manual*, 2nd ed. (Seattle: The Mountaineers Books, 2005), 13.

3. John Ortberg, interview by Tyler Reagan, *Catalyst* podcast, ep. 273, May 2, 2014, http://catalyst.libsyn.com/john-ortberg-chris-cauley-episode-273.

4. Allison Vesterfelt, *Packing Light: Thoughts on Living with Less Baggage* (Chicago: Moody Press, 2013), 130.

5. Blaine Eldredge, *Killing Lions: A Guide Through the Trials Young Men Face* (Nashville: Thomas Nelson, 2016),159.

6. Alberto Salazar, *14 Minutes: A Running Legend's Life and Death and Life* (New York: Rodale, 2012), 29.

7. Natalie Goldberg, *The True Secret of Writing: Connecting Life with Language* (New York: Atria, 2013), 41–41.

8. *The Daily Bible* (Eugene, OR: Harvest House, 1984).

9. Eric Weiner, *Man Seeks God: My Flirtations with the Divine* (New York: Hachette, 2011), audio CD.

10. Twitter exchange with Clark Moreland, June 14, 2014.

11. Erwin McManus, *Wide Awake: The Future Is Waiting Within You* (Nashville: Thomas Nelson, 2008), 5.

12. Nancy Ortberg, interview by *Catalyst* podcast, ep. 238, August 22, 2013, http://catalyst.libsyn.com/nancy-ortberg-seth-condrey-episode-238.

13. *Jeff Galloway's Blog*; "Benefits of Walk Breaks on Long Runs," blog entry by Jeff Galloway, April 7, 2014, http://jeffgalloway.typepad.com/jeff_galloways_blog/2014/04/benefits-of-walk-breaks-on-long-runs-.html.

14. *Patrick Morley* (blog); "How My View on Spiritual Disciplines Has Changed," blog entry by Patrick Morley, December 20, 2015, http://patrickmorley.com/blog/f9a7e45f-14a9-4da8-b689-1ac16ba2da14.

15. Erwin McManus, *The Artisan Soul: Crafting Your Soul into a Work of Art* (New York: HarperOne, 2014), 32.

16. George Sheehan MD, *The Essential Sheehan: A Lifetime of Running Wisdom from the Legendary Dr. George Sheehan* (New York: Rodale, 2013) 87.

17. McManus, *Artisan Soul*, 32.

18. Philip Nation, *Habits for Holiness: How the Spiritual Disciplines Grow Us Up, Draw Us Together, and Send Us Out* (Chicago: Moody Publishers, 2016),

19. Rebekah Lerner, comment during a yoga workshop in Cortona, Italy, 2015.

20. John Ortberg, interview by Charles Lee, *Catalyst* podcast, ep. 243, September 13, 2013, http://catalyst.libsyn.com/john-ortberg-gary-haugen-pranitha-timothy-episode-243.

21. Leonard Sweet, *What Matters Most: How We Got the Point but Missed the Person* (Colorado Springs: WaterBrook, 2004), 10.

22. McManus, *Artisan Soul,* 142.

23. John Ortberg, "No More Mr. Nice Group," CT Pastors, *Christianity Today,* summer 2005, http://www.christianitytoday.com/pastors/2005/summer/13.35.html.

24. Alain de Botton, Twitter post, March 4, 2015 (11:08 AM).

25. Gordon MacDonald, *A Resilient Life: You Can Move Ahead No Matter What* (Nashville: Thomas Nelson, 2004),191.

26. McManus, *Artisan Soul,* 142.

27. Natalie Goldberg, *True Secret of Writing,* 142.

28. Paul Arden, *It's Not How Good You Are, It's How Good You Want to Be: The World's Best Selling Book by Paul Arden* (London: Phaedon), 2003), quoted in Austin Kleon, *Show Your Work! 10 Ways to Share Your Creativity and Get Discovered* (New York: Workman, 2014), 72.

29. Mark Batterson, *Wild Goose Chase: Reclaim the Adventure of Pursuing God* (Colorado Springs: Multnomah, 2008), 3.

30. John Gribbin, *Deep Simplicity: Bringing Order to Chaos and Complexity* (New York: Random House, 2004), 111.

31. Patricia Ryan Madson, *Improv Wisdom: Don't Prepare, Just Show Up* (New York: Crown, 2005), 82.

32. Jay Griffiths, *Savage Grace: A Journey in Wildness* (Berkely: Counterpoint, 2015).

33. Quote taken from the motion picture *The Hobbit: An Unexpected Journey*, pt. 1 of the film series The Hobbit, Peter Jackson, dir., 2012. Based on the fantasy novel *The Hobbit* by J. R. R. Tolkien, 1937.

34. Kleon, *Show Your Work!*, 197.

35. Mark Batterson, *In a Pit with a Lion on a Snowy Day: How to Survive and Thrive When Opportunity Roars* (Colorado Springs: Multnomah, 2006), 85.

36. Jonathan Acuff, from his Instagram, https://www.instagram.com/p/YIrpg/.

37. Erwin McManus, *Uprising: A Revolution of the Soul*, (Nashville: Thomas Nelson, 2003), 97.

38. Garlinda Burton, Marjourie Suchocki, and Martin E. Mary, *The Upper Room Disciplines 2003: A Book of Daily Devotions* (Nashville: Upper Room, 2002), 13.

39. Batterson, *Wild Goose Chase*, 2. Order of sentences in quote reversed.

40. William Blake, *The Complete Poetry and Prose of William Blake*, rev. ed., David Erdman, ed., foreword and commentary by Harold Bloom (Berkely: University of California Press, 2008), 511.

41. Jon Acuff, *Start: Punch Fear in the Face, Escape Average, Do Work That Matters* (Brentwood, TN: Lampo Press, 2013), 68.

42. Howard G. Hendricks, from the foreword to Walter A. Henrichsen, *Disciples Are Made Not Born: How to Help Others Grow to Maturity in Christ* (Colorado Springs: Cook Communications, 1974).

43. Bob Goff, Twitter post, October 29, 2013.

44. Quotes taken from the motion picture *The Fellowship of the Ring*, pt. 1 of the film series The Lord of the Rings, Peter Jackson, dir., 2001. Based on *The Fellowship of the Ring*, bk. 1 in The Lord of the Rings trilogy by J. R. R. Tolkien, 1954.

45. Henrichsen, *Disciples Are Made Not Born*, 8.

46. MacDonald, *A Resilient Life*, 17.

47. McManus, *Artisan Soul*, 142.

48. Yvon Chouinard, *Let My People Go Surfing: The Education of a Reluctant Businessman* (New York: Penguin, 2005), 90.

49. Peter Matthiessen, *The Snow Leopard* (New York: Penguin, 1978), 107.

50. John Maeda, *The Laws of Simplicity: Design, Technology, Business, Life* (Cambridge: MIT Press, 2006), 89.

51. "Ultralight Backpacking Basics," REI website, accessed April 7, 2016, https://www.rei.com/learn/expert-advice/ultralight-backpacking.html.

52. Mark Sanborn, "8 Differences Between Your Resume and Your Legacy," accessed April 14, 2015, http://www.marksanborn.com/blog/8-differences-resume-legacy/.

53. Annie Dillard, *Three by Annie Dillard: Pilgrim at Tinker Creek, An American Childhood, The Writing Life* (New York: HarperCollins, 1990), 597.

54. *Denison Forum* (blog); "Are There Rewards in Heaven?," blog entry by Jim Denison, July 28, 2011, https://www.denisonforum.org/faith-questions/salvation/are-there-rewards-in-heaven/.

55. Seth Godin's blog; "Are You Willing to Build a Trail?," blog entry by Seth Godin, September 8, 2014, http://sethgodin.typepad.com/seths_blog/2014/09/are-you-willing-to-work-hard-enough-to-get-work.html.

56. Mike Foster, *Gracenomics: Unleash the Power of Second Chance Living* (Matthews, NC: People of the Second Chance, 2010), 51.

57. Linda Ronstadt, *Simple Dreams: A Musical Memoir* (New York: Simon & Schuster, 2013), 192.

58. Vesterfelt, *Packing Light*, 134.

59. Ibid., 188.

60. Quote taken from the motion picture *Something to Talk About*, Lasse Hallstrom, dir., 1995.

61. Leroy Eims, *The Lost Art of Disciple Making* (Grand Rapids: Zondervan, 1978), 52.

CPSIA information can be obtained
at www.ICGtesting.com
Printed in the USA
LVOW07s2135171217
560113LV00006B/579/P